Twenty-five years on twenty estates

Twenty–five years on twenty estates

Turning the tide?

Rebecca Tunstall and Alice Coulter

JOSEPH ROWNTREE
FOUNDATION

First published in Great Britain in November 2006 by

The Policy Press
Fourth Floor, Beacon House
Queen's Road
Bristol BS8 1QU
UK

Tel no   +44 (0)117 331 4054
Fax no   +44 (0)117 331 4093
Email   tpp-info@bristol.ac.uk
www.policypress.org.uk

Published for the Joseph Rowntree Foundation by The Policy Press

10-digit ISBN 1 86134 935 1
13-digit ISBN 978 1 86134 935 4

British Library Cataloguing in Publication Data
A catalogue record for this book is available from the British Library.

Library of Congress Cataloging-in-Publication Data
A catalog record for this book has been requested.

Rebecca Tunstall is a lecturer in housing at the London School of Economics and Political Science.
Alice Coulter was until recently a research officer at the London School of Economics and Political
Science.

The **Joseph Rowntree Foundation** has supported this project as part of its programme of research and
innovative development projects, which it hopes will be of value to policy makers, practitioners and
service users. The facts presented and views expressed in this report are, however, those of the authors
and not necessarily those of the Foundation.

Cover image supplied by www.third-avenue.co.uk
Cover design by Qube Design Associates, Bristol
Printed in Great Britain by Latimer Trend, Plymouth

Contents

List of figures

List of tables

Acknowledgements

We would like to thank Helen Beck, who carried out all the street interviews. Jonathan Brearley, Jackie Haq, Pat Maddocks, Bert Provan, Jim Ripley, Max Steinberg, Helena Tunstall and Rebekah Widdowfield provided very helpful comments at advisory group meetings and on project drafts. Anne Power at the London School of Economics and Political Science provided essential continuity with previous studies on the 20 estates. Katharine Knox of the Joseph Rowntree Foundation provided invaluable support and ideas throughout the project, from conception to final draft. All the photographs were taken by Alice Coulter and Rebecca Tunstall.

Above all, we would like to thank the 158 staff and residents of the 20 estates who gave their time in 2004 and 2005, and the staff and residents who have contributed to previous rounds of the research over the past 25 years.

Summary

This report is based on four successive pieces of research carried out over a 25-year project on 20 'unpopular' council estates in England. Most of the estates were relatively successful after they were first built, but by 1980 they were unpopular, had serious management problems with poor services, many empty homes and unkempt environments, and many also had significant physical problems. The estates were chosen for research in the early 1980s because at that time the councils that owned and managed them were introducing improvement initiatives, based on local housing management with increased resident involvement. The estates include every major type of council housing, from 1920s semi-detached homes to 1970s modernist estates, and are located in London, the Midlands, the North East and North West of England. Overall, they typify less popular council estates, which have been symbols of housing and urban problems and targets of policy for every government over the past 25 years. The estates have been tracked through visits and interviews in 1982, 1988, 1994 and 2005. This latest report comments on their progress over that period, with a focus on the last 10 years.

Key changes in the estates, 1980–2005

According to staff and residents' assessments in 1988, 1995 and 2005, six of the 20 estates saw steady improvements over the 25-year period. By 2005, a resident in one estate said: "This estate is the pride of the local authority". Ten more estates had experienced some threats or reverses to progress at some point, but had seen improvements to 1995 and further improvements by 2005. A senior manager in one of these estates said: "It's right easy now, housing officers don't know they've been born! It was Beirut!". In the four remaining estates, the position in 2005 was uncertain. In one, improvements had appeared at risk in 1995, and by 2005 it had declined: a resident said: "It's a dump and that's being polite". Two estates were subject to plans for dramatic redevelopments, after earlier initiatives had failed to resolve physical problems and poor reputations. In the last site, a major redevelopment in the 1990s failed to overcome the estate's problems, and a senior manager said: "The profile is similar to what it was 10 years ago ... it has continued to cause concern".

What contributed to these mainly very positive assessments? Over the past 25 years, the estates have been affected by a complex mix of mainstream housing policy, government regeneration initiatives targeted at less popular estates, and the actions of councils, Registered Social Landlords (RSLs) and residents. They have also felt the effects of broader social and economic trends, which over the past 10 years, for example, have included falling unemployment, falling crime and rising school performance. Untangling the causes of these changes is very difficult, as many factors have operated together, and change of one kind often has knock-on effects that can lead to other changes. Major factors include: physical investment and redevelopment, management reorganisation and improvement in management performance and the development of mixed tenure on the estates. Popularity gains and changes in the profile of estate populations have also been evident across the estates.

Most of the estates received several different types of central government regeneration funding over 25 years. For example, nine estates received Estate Action funds and nine were within areas that received Single Regeneration Budget funding – both schemes initiated under Conservative governments – while eight estates had local Sure Starts and three were in New Deal for Communities areas, both Labour Government programmes. Central government funding was important to deliver the dramatic redevelopments that took place in six areas, involving a mixture of demolition of council homes, new building by private developers and RSLs, and some sales of council homes. Such funding also paid for basic refurbishment and improvement to many homes – some built in the early years of the 20th century – for example, replacing roofs and wiring, as well as improving estate environments. Local authorities also contributed their own funds. Increasingly restricted, over the past 10 years they have sought routes to investment including passing ownership to RSLs and responsibility for management to new Arms' Length Management Organisations (ALMOs) set up by councils. Increasingly, estates were financing their own redevelopments though sale of land and new building.

Throughout the 25 years, successive governments have pressured local authorities to reorganise and improve their housing management, for example, encouraging decentralisation and resident involvement, the Conservatives' introduction of Compulsory Competitive Tendering of service delivery and Labour's Best Value performance management regime, and introducing new managers, including RSLs and ALMOs. In 1995, 18 of the estates were managed by councils, but by 2005 only nine remained under council management. Three estates were owned by RSLs, which had taken over management. Seven were run by ALMOs, and one was managed by a private sector contractor. Local estate-based management signalled the start of improvement efforts in the estates 25 years earlier, and staff and residents saw local management as essential to the progress seen up to the mid-1990s. However, by 2005, only half the estates had local estate-based or area offices, and some estates were managed centrally, with residents contacting staff mainly via call centres. Recentralisation was due to pressures for efficiency, in some cases, triggered by the arrival of new managers, the availability of new technology, and a perception that problems in estates had reduced.

Over the past 25 years, performance in the estates has improved markedly, evident in the reductions in empty homes, the end of neglected, rubbish-strewn environments, and, in most cases, speedier housing repairs services. Some residents' groups were involved in management and regeneration initiatives in the estates in 2005, and in two sites, Tenant Management Organisations were responsible for estate management. However, only 14 estates had active residents' groups in 2005, compared with 18 in 1995.

In 1995, the report on developments from 1980-95 (Power and Tunstall, 1995) referred to the 20 as 'unpopular council estates', but changes since 1995 mean that this is no longer accurate. From a situation of unpopularity and stigma in 1980, demand for the estates in absolute terms and relative to other local options rose between 1980 and 1995, and continued to increase during the next 10 years. By 2005, vacancy rates had fallen to local authority and national averages for social housing. None of the estates was seen by managers as 'difficult to let' (Figure 4), decades of stigma connected in some estates to slum clearance had faded, there was moderate demand for homes in most cases, and three estates had even reached 'high-demand' status.

While, in 1980, all the homes in the estates were council-owned, housing tenure in estates gradually become more diverse, with change accelerating after 1995 (Figures 7-9). By 2005, social housing made up an average of 81% of homes across the estates. This was not all council housing, and in three estates all the social rented homes had been transferred from councils to RSLs. In six estates, there were dramatic redevelopments, mostly after 1995, involving a mixture of demolition of council homes, new building by private developers and RSLs, and some sales of council homes to developers. These added 11% home ownership to estates overall. Take-up of the Right to Buy (RTB), introduced in 1980, was very slow for the first 15 years of the policy in the estates compared with their local authorities and the national average, but accelerated after 2000 to account for an average of 9% of the homes in the estates by 2005. Between 1981 and 1991, concentrations of unemployed residents, children and lone-parent households increased sharply in the estates. By 1995, managers and residents felt that the pressure of polarisation was threatening progress. However, dramatically, most of these trends reversed in 1991-2001. The gaps between the estate populations and their local authorities and the nations as a whole decreased on unemployment rates (Figure 26) and employment rates. The concentrations of young people and lone-parent households also decreased, suggesting that the populations in the estates in 2005 were not as disadvantaged as at the time of the past studies. These changes are likely to be due to a mixture of changes in the people living in the estates and changes in the circumstances of individuals.

Performance at estate-linked secondary schools, a key government neighbourhood renewal target, improved significantly between 1994 and 2004, and the gaps between these schools, their local education authorities and the nation reduced (Figure 23). Attendance rates also improved faster for estate-linked schools. These schools did not necessarily educate a majority of estate children and estate children did not necessarily make up a majority of school rolls.

Crime had also been a major concern for residents and managers in the 1980s and early 1990s, but its salience reduced significantly by 2005. One resident said: "Crime is not a big issue, not compared to what it was 10 years ago".

However, while these areas showed progress, levels of economic inactivity had increased in the estates, going against the national trend, and suggesting that the fall in unemployment may have been partly due to people leaving the labour market. Residents' health was also significantly worse than the average for estates' local authorities or the nation as a whole. In addition, anti-social behaviour had to some extent replaced crime as a significant concern for residents and staff.

Closing the gaps and becoming more 'normal' areas

Over the past 25 years, the gaps in outcomes between the 20 estates and their local authorities and the nation reduced in terms of two key neighbourhood renewal targets: employment and unemployment rates; and achievement at estate-linked schools. The estates also saw progress in terms of increased popularity, changes in tenure mix and the physical form, condition, appearance and maintenance of homes.

These formerly very unpopular estates have become more 'normal' as majority social housing areas, in terms of popularity, the mix of tenure and landlords, the level of management decentralisation, and management performance. By 2005, they were close to the national average for social housing in terms of residents' satisfaction with their homes, landlord and area, and levels of employment, unemployment and economic activity. One manager said that in 1995, "the main aim was to get control of the estate, and then to normalise the conditions and practices" – this had been achieved over 10 years. Another said that by 2005 his estate was, "very, very quiet, almost run of the mill". Meanwhile, however, the total amount of council housing has halved, and social housing as a whole has become more marginalised. In 1981, more heads of social renting households were employed than were economically inactive, but by 2004, more than twice as many were inactive as were employed.

Explaining the changes

In 1995, research on the 20 estates concluded that progress over the first 15 years could be attributed to a combination of sustained local housing management, periodic capital investment and resident involvement. By 2005, progress had continued, and these factors still appeared important, but the explanation is more complex.

Vicious circles or 'spirals of decline' can set in for deprived neighbourhoods, and these were certainly operating in the 20 estates in 1980. By 2005, however, most estates were instead showing at least some virtuous circles, creating complex but positive knock-on effects, so, for example, increasing popularity could reduce the difficulty of management, and increase the likelihood of less deprived residents applying for homes.

In all the estates, regeneration funding and other capital expenditure has been an important part of sustained improvements in conditions, popularity and resident satisfaction. Investment and redevelopment also had other knock-on effects, such as cutting the number of estates with design features that made them hard to manage and prone to crime. The estates with the least investment stagnated in the 1990s after earlier progress. In some cases, limited results from early investment led to more dramatic initiatives. Dramatic redevelopment led to significant improvements in five of the six estates where it was tried. In the sixth, mixed tenure become a problem rather than a protection, as homes intended for low-cost home ownership failed to find a market and led to a large, high-turnover and hard-to-manage private rented sector in the estate.

Local, intensive and improved management and the involvement of resident groups appeared to be important to improvements and to trouble shooting throughout the 25 years. However, by 2005, the connection between local management, resident involvement and improved estate trajectories weakened, because in some improved estates, landlords withdrew local management and residents' groups faded, as part of the 'normalisation' process.

In addition to national policy, other factors outside the estates appeared to be having greater influence over them from the late 1990s. National and regional trends, including rising employment, increasing house prices and demand for social housing and other types of housing introduced on to the estates such as owner-occupied housing, falling crime and rising educational achievement were important to recent changes in many of the estates. However, local factors including the improvement of estate reputations, investment in homes and spending on crime prevention measures helped the estates to benefit from these wider trends.

Has the tide turned?

In 1995, it appeared that the 20 estates were 'swimming against the tide', with improvements potentially threatened by increased social polarisation. Overall, by 2005, the findings for the estates appeared very positive, suggesting additional progress over the past 10 years. There are also some signs of significant and sustainable improvements, suggesting the estates may be 'turning the tide'. These include not just the continued years of progress, but also the apparent ending to some long-lasting problems, the creation of virtuous circles, and 'normalisation'.

However, there are major cautions for interpretation and for policy. First, despite the reduction in gaps between the estates and their local authorities and the nation, significant differences remain. For example, while the gap between unemployment rates in the estates overall and for England as a whole fell from 25% in 1991 to 11% in 2001, the estate rate was still three times the national level in 2001. In 2001, in its National Strategy for Neighbourhood Renewal, the government pledged to end gaps between different areas, so that 'within 10-20 years, no-one should be seriously disadvantaged by where they live' (SEU, 2001, p 8). If the estates were significantly disadvantaging the people who lived in them in 1980, this was still the case in 2005. The experience of the past 25 years shows that it is possible to make progress over the long term, but narrowing the gaps takes sustained commitments of capital funding, revenue funding and attention from central government, landlords and housing managers and residents' groups. Fully closing the gaps to end significant disadvantage is likely to take more than 10 or 20 years.

Second, improvements achieved in these estates are unlikely to be sustainable without ongoing support. Progress over the past 25 years was not straightforward, and 14 estates saw some threats to progress during the period, while, in 2005, four faced uncertain futures. Improvements are not necessarily secure. Achievements could also be threatened by 'normalisation' leading to, for example, reduced priority for central government support and landlord attention, and less local management. Major physical and tenure change did not guarantee improvement, and even where it was successful, staff and residents were anxious for careful management to prevent, for example, the emergence of drugs problems. Some of the improvements also appear to be linked to wider social and economic trends, such as strong housing and labour markets, which may not continue. One senior manager said: "The market is changing faster than ever before ... it could change in another way in the future".

Given that the 20 estates are increasingly typical of social housing and majority social housing areas, these points apply not just to a minority of more difficult estates, but across the national social housing stock.

Finally, this study is about places, not individual people. While almost all of the estates are now significantly better places to live than they were in 1980 or in 1995, the lives of individual residents may not necessarily have changed for the better. At least some of the changes in social composition of the estates are due to movements of people in and out of the estates rather than changes in the situation of individual people. Some of the changes in population may be due to disadvantaged people leaving these estates, and both mixed tenure and increased popularity may also make it more difficult for the most disadvantaged to gain homes in the improved estates.

Introduction

1. Twenty-five years on 20 estates: a unique study

This report is based on research carried out on 20 unpopular council estates in England over a 25-year period, which set out to examine the changing conditions and situation of these estates. The estates have been tracked through visits and interviews in 1982, 1988, 1994 and 2005. This report covers the whole 25-year period, with a focus on changes in the past 10 years[1]. The study allows an unusual long-term assessment of the cumulative impact of housing policy, other policy and social and economic changes, operating at national and neighbourhood level, on a group of less popular council estates and their residents, over a period of major change in policy and society.

While a majority of social housing residents would like to own a home one day, most are satisfied with their homes and neighbourhoods. Social housing estates that are a significant problem to those who live in them, and those who manage them – 'difficult to let', 'difficult to live in', or, in more headline-grabbing terms, 'sink estates' – have been and remain a small part of the UK housing system. Estimates and measures have varied over time and according to definitions used, and are not necessarily robust or comparable, but in both 1980 and 2005 just 5% of council housing was described as 'difficult to let' in reports (Burbidge et al, 1981; ODPM, 2005, table 104) to central government, up to 25% was located in 'deprived estates' in 1991, according to a survey by Price Waterhouse (1997), and in 2003, up to 19% of 'predominantly council-built areas' were suffering from 'liveability problems', according to the Survey of English Housing (ODPM, 2003a).

However, over the past 25 years, these problematic estates have influenced public and political attitudes to social housing out of proportion to their prevalence. Since 1997, under the Labour government, these kinds of estates have been pointed out as the most obvious place to find social exclusion, and have acted as a handy symbol of a concept that is sometimes hard to understand. They have also been seen as part of the cause of deprivation, social exclusion and other problems, including crime, although the evidence for this is limited, and other kinds of neighbourhoods can also be unpopular and have deprived residents. These estates have been subject to many special policy initiatives since the 1980s, but they have also probably affected mainstream policy both to improve and reduce the whole council and social housing sector.

The research in these estates covers 25 years of housing policy, other central government policy, and changes and initiatives in local government. The long-lasting domination of the Conservative party has been replaced by new and unprecedented Labour party control at national level. Housing policy changes include deregulation and liberalisation for most parts of the housing system, and restructuring of social housing subsidy from supply to demand side, and assets from local authorities into private and housing association hands. The salience of housing policy and expenditure on it has reduced. This been only partly offset by government interest in, and expenditure on, regeneration and neighbourhood renewal, which has been targeted at less popular estates and other deprived areas, including some of the estates considered here.

---

1 Detail on developments from the late 1970s to 1995 can be found in the previous reports in this series: Power, 1984; Power, 1991; Power and Tunstall, 1995.

In addition, over the 25 years, almost any other conceivable contextual factor has also changed significantly. Popular culture of the 1980s is now often seen as an almost-exotic object of nostalgia or amusement, but many aspects of social and economic life have changed as much. For example, to be a lone parent was more than twice as common in 2005 as in 1980, as was being a degree holder. Crime victimisation almost doubled between 1981 and 1995, but then fell back to about 1981 levels. Educational participation beyond 16 and beyond 18 has increased. Life expectancy has increased and the length of healthy life has increased faster, although some health inequalities have grown. The population has aged, and become more ethnically diverse. Household structures have changed, with increasing proportions of single-adult households, unmarried couples and multi-adult households as well as lone parents. Incomes have increased, partly fuelling the growth of home ownership. All of these changes influence the pressures on the housing system and the role of less popular estates within it.

Social, economic and political change is likely to be part of the explanation for changes in the estates. It also provides a shifting yardstick for assessing conditions, whether for current or potential residents or policy makers or researchers, who all look at these estates in the context of different expectations and options.

2. Development and decline: the 20 estates from origins to 1980

The group of 20 estates in this study includes some from each major stage of English council housing development. Eight of the estates had been built in the 1930s, two in the 1940s, three in the 1940s and 1950s, three in the 1960s and three in the 1970s (Table 1). In 1980, seven of the estates were made up mostly of houses and six were mostly made up of low-rise flats of traditional construction, while seven were mostly medium- and high-rise flats of non-traditional construction and layout. They ranged in size from about 300 homes to nearly 2,000. They are located in local authorities across the most urbanised regions of England. Map 1 shows the location of the estates and a series of photographs follow that show the different types of housing in the estates.

Table 1: Basic characteristics of the 20 estates

Estate code	Location	Built form	Date completed	Number of homes covered by initiative at start
1	London	Low-rise traditional flats	1940s	559
2	London	Medium- and high-rise non-traditional flats	1970s	812
3	London	Medium- and high-rise non-traditional flats	1970s	1,063
4	London	Medium-rise non-traditional flats	1970s	1,500
5	North East	Houses – including non-traditional construction	1940s-1950s	1,000
6	North West	Medium-rise non-traditional flats	1960s-1970s	1,014
7	London	Low-rise traditional flats	1930s	1,350
8	London	Low-rise traditional flats	1930s	882
9	London	Low-rise traditional flats	1930s	272
10	London	Low-rise traditional flats	1950s	698
11	London	Medium- and high-rise non-traditional flats	1960s	1,114
12	London	Medium-rise non-traditional flats	1960s	1,849
13	North East	Houses	1940s	393
14	North West	Houses	1930s	312
15	North West	Low-rise traditional flats	1950s	1,930
16	East Midlands	Houses	1930s	1,975
17	London	Medium- and high-rise non-traditional flats	1970s	1,898
18	North East	Houses	1920s-1930s	1,000
19	North West	Houses	1930s	473
20	West Midlands	Houses	1930s	350

Note: The estate codes, numbers from 1 to 20, are used to refer to individual estates in the text. The codes have been allocated to indicate the trajectories of the estates over the period 1980-2005 (see Table 3).

Locations of the 20 estates

1,114 homes including flats in high-rise blocks and maisonettes in low-rise blocks, built in the 1960s in London, estate 11

1,063 flats in medium- and high-rise blocks built in the 1970s in London, estate 3

882 flats in low-rise traditional blocks built in the 1930s, estate 8

1,000 houses of traditional and non-traditional construction built in the 1940s and 1950s in the North East, estate 5

312 houses built in the 1930s in the North West, estate 14

1,975 houses built in the 1930s in the East Midlands, estate 16

By the late 1970s, some of the 20 estates had been in existence for 50 years, while some had been completed for less than a decade. Some of the older estates were stigmatised from the start by a link to slum clearance schemes, and there were problems making the very first lettings of homes in some of the estates completed in the 1960s and 1970s, but, on the whole, many of the 20 were initially fairly popular. However, staff and residents described how the physical conditions and reputations of the estates declined over time. By 1980, the 20 estates each faced a series of problems, from neglected, rubbish-strewn environments to concentrations of poor and more vulnerable social groups (Table 2). These problems led their local authorities to start experimental estate-based housing management initiatives, one in 1970, with the remaining 19 estates taking action over the period 1979-82. The 20 estates are located in, and were owned by, a total of 18 local authorities, as two local authorities each had two estates. The 20 estates were not specifically chosen to form a representative sample of unpopular council estates in 1980, but in fact, for being atypical, because of having these management initiatives. Nevertheless, the group shared features with unpopular estates in a national government study carried out by Burbidge and colleagues (1981), including the size, age, design and type of local authority in which they were located.

3. 'Swimming against the tide': key changes in the estates, 1980–95

The report (Power and Tunstall, 1995) summing up key changes in the estates 1980-95 concluded that almost all of the 20 estates had been restored from the most extreme social, physical and management problems seen at the start of the 1980s. By 1994, residents and staff on most estates believed that conditions had improved, and only five estates were still considered by staff to be difficult to let. Staff and residents were enthusiastic about the locally-based services that had evolved over the period. Table 2 describes changes over the period 1980-95 in more detail.

Table 2: Estate characteristics leading to the establishment of estate-based management initiatives, and changes by 1995

Characteristics	Start of initiatives in the late 1970s and early 1980s	1995
Neglected, rubbish-strewn environment	20	1
Poor repairs and maintenance	19	7
High level of crime and vandalism	19	9
Rent arrears above local authority average for council housing	16	13
Lone-parent households above local authority average	16	20
Unemployment and benefit claiming above local authority average	16	20
Difficult to let	15	5
Proportion of children above local authority average	15	20
Proportion of homes empty above local authority average for council housing	14	10
Little community involvement	14	7
Isolated location with few shopping or social facilities	11	11
Structural problems	10	6
Minority ethnic population above local authority average	9	10
Difficult to manage and unpopular design	7	6
Continuing stigma of first allocations for slum clearance areas	6	5

Sources: Power, 1984; Power and Tunstall, 1995

By 1995:

- Seven estates had improved over the previous 15 years and appeared to be stable.
- Five had improved but changes were at risk.
- Four had improved but were in decline again, and one of these was in a state of crisis with high levels of crime and many empty homes.
- Four had improved but then stalled or declined, and dramatic redevelopments had been proposed.

Improvements in the estates' position appeared to be due to three main factors:

- Decentralised and intensive housing management and the efforts of staff.
- Residents' involvement in housing management and other activities; and
- Periodic investment by local authorities and central government in most estates.

In 1995, 17 of the 20 estates had at least two of these factors in place and had done so for most or all of the 15 preceding years. Where one or more were missing, progress was more likely to be at risk.

Some of the original problems that had sparked initiatives in the 1970s and 1980s remained in some estates in 1995 (Table 2). In addition, concentrations of unemployment, lone parenthood, minority ethnic groups and young people were actually significantly greater at the start of the 1990s than when initiatives began. Concentrations of deprivation and residents with restricted choice in the housing market reflected the increasingly polarised position of social housing overall, as well as these estates' continuing relative unpopularity. Residents felt pressured by crime and social problems and managers found controlling socially disruptive behaviour increasingly difficult. Fifteen years' experience showed that large housing estates could be better run from a local base and that conditions could improve with targeted staff and investment, even where the population was very disadvantaged. However, overall, in 1995 the 20 estates were 'swimming against the tide'.

Commenting on less popular social housing in 1998, Tony Blair stated: 'Over the last two decades the gap between these "worst estates" and the rest of the country has grown.... It shames us as a nation, it wastes lives and we all have to pay the costs of dependency and social division' (SEU, 1998, p 2).

4. The key questions for 1995-2005

In the light of the progress seen in the estates over the first 15 years of the study, the key questions for the research covering the most recent 10 years are:

- Have improvements made in 1980-95 been maintained?
- Have there been further gains from 1995 to 2005?
- What has happened to the estates that were in decline, in crisis or facing uncertainty 10 years ago?
- What impact has mainstream housing policy had on the estates? What impact have regeneration and neighbourhood renewal policies had?
- Have these estates benefited from the strong economy and increases in employment seen across the UK in the past decade?
- What other factors explain changes in the estates?
- Have the gaps between the estates and their local authorities and the nation identified in previous studies reduced?

- Has progress developed far enough and achieved enough stability so that the tide has turned?
- What are the lessons for other areas?

5. Research methods

A mixed research method approach was used to address the above questions and consider progress on the estates. In 2005, a total of 41 visits were made to the estates themselves, with a total of 158 interviews in the estates and at other locations. Similar data were collected in similar ways to previous studies, to enable continued longitudinal comparison (Power, 1984, 1991; Power and Tunstall, 1995). For each estate, with one exception, the team:

- Interviewed local housing managers.
- Interviewed senior housing staff, such as directors of local authority housing departments or chief executives of registered social landlords and arm's length management organisations.
- Held detailed discussions with residents' groups (where they existed).

In one exceptional estate, plans for a dramatic redevelopment led to local controversy, and this in turn led to the local authority not allowing its staff to speak to researchers.

In addition to the above methods, very brief street interviews were carried out with about 10 residents who were not involved in groups in half of the estates, including estates without groups, estates with less active groups, and those with none. Information from residents' groups and residents' street interviews are labelled separately.

Secondary data, such as housing and regeneration strategy documents, Audit Commission inspection reports, and newsletters were gathered and analysed. The censuses of 1981, 1991 and 2001 were used for information on the populations of the estates. As in previous rounds, interviewees were promised that neither the estates nor they as individuals should be identifiable from the research. This was intended to help gain access, to promote frankness, and to protect the areas from potentially stigmatising publicity.

For more information on the research methods, see the Appendix.

// Changes in the estates, 1995-2005

This chapter examines staff and resident assessments of progress on the 20 estates and sets out the main changes in the estates behind these assessments in more detail. The main issues covered include:

- Estate popularity
- Estate ownership
- Social housing management
- Regeneration and investment
- Crime and anti-social behaviour
- Facilities, activities and residents' groups
- Schools
- Estate populations

In each case, the possible causes and the relative impact of changes are examined, considering policy issues and social and economic factors. Both the national context and factors at local and estate level are considered. Changes in many of the areas are likely to themselves act as further catalysts for change and may cause knock-on effects on other issues, making exact cause and effect difficult to disentangle.

6. Staff and resident assessments of progress

Local housing managers and residents were asked to consider how much the estates had improved over the long term. Half of local housing managers interviewed in 1995 felt estate conditions had improved since 1988. By 2005, nearly three quarters thought that trends over the past decade had been positive (Figure 1).

Figure 1: Housing managers' views of trends in estate conditions

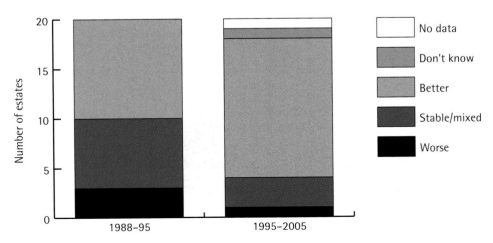

Sources: Interviews, 1995, 2005

Only one manager said the estate had worsened over the decade, due to increases in graffiti and anti-social behaviour (estate 19). Less than half felt there had been improvements during 1995-2000, but again, very few felt there had been any decline.

As in 1995, in 2005, residents' assessments were less positive than those of managers. Nevertheless, where data were available, residents' group members were at least as positive about changes over the past 10 years as these groups had been about change in the late 1980s and early 1990s (Figure 2). Only one residents' group thought things had got worse (estate 19).

Figure 2: Residents' group members' views of trends in estate conditions

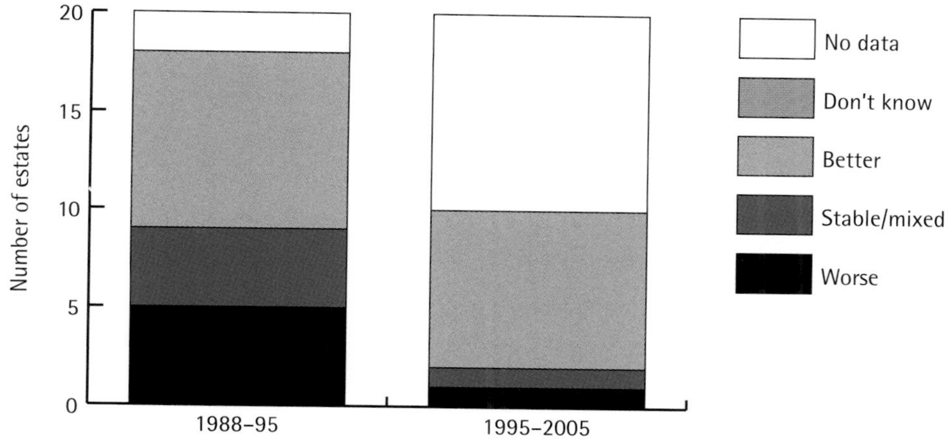

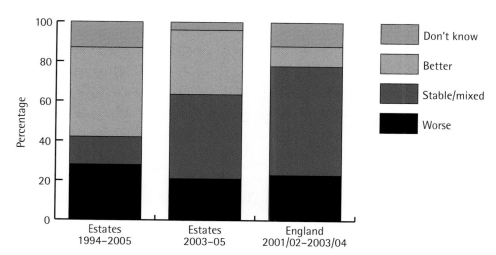

Sources: Interviews with residents' groups, 1995, 2005

Residents interviewed in the street were less positive than residents' group members, with over a quarter identifying a decline in conditions over the past decade, but they were more positive about short-term trends than the average for people in England as a whole in national surveys of estate conditions (Figure 3).

Figure 3: Residents' views of trends in estate conditions

Sources: ODPM, 2005; street interviews in 10 estates, 2005

Table 3: Trajectories of the 20 estates, 1980–2005

Trajectory	Number of estates	Estate codes
Improvements 1988-95, 1995-2005	6	1, 2, 3, 4, 5, 6
Some threats or reverses 1988-95, improvements 1995-2005	10	7, 8, 9, 10, 11, 12 13, 14, 15, 16
Other	4	17, 18, 19, 20

Sources: Power and Tunstall, 1995; interviews, 2005

Staff, residents' groups, and other residents' assessments of trends and future prospects from 1994 and 2005 were combined to describe the trajectories of the individual estates from 1988 to 2005 (Table 3).

Estate codes have been allocated to indicate into which group each estate falls.

Six of the 20 estates had ongoing positive trajectories, with improvements over 1988-95 followed by more improvements or at least by stability from 1995 to 2005 (estates 1, 2, 3, 4, 5, 6): "This estate is the pride of the local authority" (resident, estate 3).

Ten more had experienced some threats or reverses to progress during the period, but by 2005 had seen further and secure improvement on the 1995 position.

- In three estates, improvements were under threat in 1995, but in the past 10 years the situation had improved or stabilised (estates 7, 9, 16): "We're seeing dreams coming true in terms of investment" (local manager, estate 7).
- Three were facing dramatic redevelopment in 1995, but have now gone through this process and improved (estates 11, 12, 15): "If I won the lottery, I wouldn't move" (resident, estate 15).
- One was in a state of crisis in 1995 but has since been redeveloped and has now improved (estate 13): "It's right easy now, housing officers don't know they've been born! It was Beirut – although we weren't allowed to say that at the time!" (senior manager, estate 13).
- A further three were in decline in 1995 but have now improved (estates 8, 10, 14).

In four more, the position in 2005 was uncertain.

- In two, improvements were under threat in 1995, but the situation did not improve in the last 10 years of the study period and by 2005 dramatic redevelopments were planned (estates 17, 20): "The estate is intransigent – it's always been seen as a bad area, even when colleagues were at school" (senior manager, estate 17).
- One more was redeveloped but did not improve and was in decline again in 2005: "The profile is similar to what it was 10 years ago ... it has continued to cause concern ... some other areas ... could partly trace their problems to the riots of the early 1990s [but it] had similar problems without riots" (senior manager, estate 18).
- The improvements in one other estate were at risk in 1995 and it had declined since: "It's a dump and that's being polite ... you're ashamed of telling people where you live. You're on the bus and you want to stay on and go straight through. It looks a right dive" (resident, estate 19).

Overall, in 2005 significantly more estates were 'improved and stable' than in 1995. The number with improvements at risk or in decline has fallen, and none of the estates was in a state of crisis.

In summary, this initial information suggests that:

- **In 16 of the 20 estates, improvements made in 1980-95 were stabilised or maintained in 1995-2005, and, in most cases, there were further improvements.**
- **Nine of the estates that were in decline, in crisis or facing uncertainty in 1995 subsequently improved, while four were still facing problems in 2005.**

The following sections explore the changes in the estates behind these overall assessments in more detail. They also discuss potential explanations for changes, any wider implications, and how changes of one kind can contribute to changes of another.

7. Estate popularity

Unpopularity, in absolute terms and relative to other local housing options, was one of the key reasons for the original development of local management initiatives in the estates (Table 2). In 1980, 14 out of the 20 estates had a higher proportion of empty homes than the average for council housing in their local authorities, 15 out of 20 were described as 'difficult to let', five estates were the least popular in their local authorities, and 11 more were among the least popular. By 1995, only half the estates had more empty homes than the local authority average, only four were seen as difficult to let, and only two were among the least popular in their local authorities.

In the vast majority of estates, by 2005, local managers felt that there had been further improvements, both in overall demand for the estates, and in their relative popularity. In two estates they felt the situation was stable (estates 9, 20), but in none did demand appear to have fallen over 10 years. The majority of local managers felt that there was now a 'moderate' level of demand for these estates. No interviewees described the whole estate as difficult to let, although in one case, a lettings moratorium was operating prior to redevelopment, and managers thought that without the moratorium the estate might well have appeared difficult to let (estate 20). A few managers described a minority of homes as relatively difficult to let, including one-bedroom homes, warden-assisted homes, bungalows and homes near an anti-social household (Figure 4).

When asked what the bad things about the estates were in 1995, a third of residents' groups mentioned estate reputation and discrimination against residents, and, in five

Figure 4: Estates considered 'difficult to let' by managers

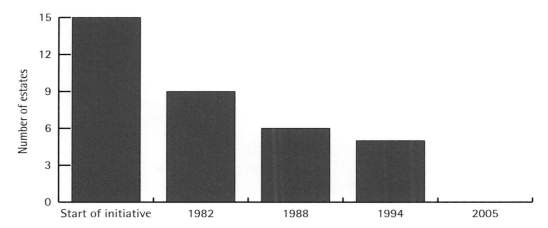

Note: In 19 estates, initiatives started in 1979–82; in one, they started in 1970.
Sources: Interviews with managers, 1982, 1988, 1994, 2005

estates, staff or residents said that there had been continuing stigma because the original development was linked to slum clearance. In contrast, in 2005, only two of the 89 residents interviewed through street interviews mentioned poor reputation, and at last the slum clearance connection, up to eight decades before, had faded.

The improvements in demand referred to by managers were reflected in a substantial drop in the proportion of homes in the 20 estates that were empty during 1995-2005 (Figure 5). During 1988-95, five estates had lettings 'crises' where the proportion of empty homes rose above 10% at some time, but in the past 10 years only three estates experienced similar episodes.

Figure 5: Proportion of estate homes empty

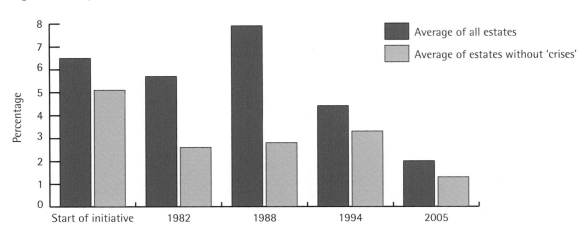

Source: Interviews with managers, 1982, 1988, 1994, 2005

Empty home, estate 14

Vacancy rates across the estates without lettings crises were close to national figures in 1988 and 1995. By 2005, overall vacancies in the estates were below national and local authority averages for council housing. Only six had levels of empty homes above local authority averages, and in three estates this was because lettings had stopped prior to demolition. Meanwhile, three estates had even managed to creep into the high-demand category (estates 6, 15, 19).

The estates also became more popular relative to other social housing options. By 2005, none of the estates was the least popular in their local authority area, and only two were among the least popular (for those where data were available) (Figure 6).

Figure 6: Popularity relative to other estates in the local authority area, according to managers

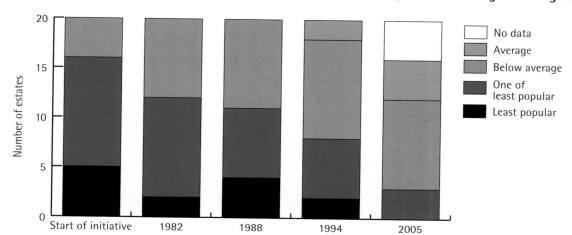

Note: In 19 estates, initiatives started 1979–82; in one, they started in 1970.
Sources: Interviews with managers, 1982, 1988, 1994, 2005

In summary, by 2005 most of the estates were not 'neighbourhoods of choice', but they cannot be described as 'unpopular estates', and were mostly close to normal for social housing in terms of popularity and demand.

The improved absolute and relative popularity of the 20 estates appears to be due to three factors:

- The knock-on effects of improvements in the estates, as identified by housing managers and residents above, and improvements in terms of housing management, physical conditions of homes and environment, crime and social conditions (see especially Sections 8-11).
- The knock-on effects of reduced supply of homes for rent in the estates through demolition and sales (see Sections 8 and 10).
- Reduced supply of social housing and general increases in demand for housing, including social housing, in the local authorities and regions in which they are located.

A national decline in social housing and rises in house prices have promoted increased demand nationwide, with knock-on effects even in lower-demand regions and less popular estates. The local authorities in which the estates are located lost 32% of their council housing between 1994 and 2003. The same processes have encouraged Right to Buy take-up even in less popular areas, accelerating the process. Within the estates, demolition has removed the least popular homes and reduced the total number of homes available by between five and 10 per cent overall, and, on average, only 81% of the remaining homes were for social renting (Section 8).

Site of homes demolished in the late 1990s, estate 5

The level of popularity relative to other housing options is not just an indicator of relative conditions, but can also cause further changes. Relative unpopularity is part of the 'spiral of decline', associated with a sifting process through which only the more disadvantaged and needy residents are likely to accept accommodation. In contrast, increasing absolute and relative popularity has the following knock-on implications:

- More competition for homes in the estates, with a tendency for more advantaged residents, those not applying as homeless and those able to wait, to be more likely to move into vacant homes, and to be more likely to stay.
- More take-up of the Right to Buy.
- Easier and less costly management, and better performance indicators, as less turnover and fewer empty properties means fewer and less difficult tasks.
- A potentially reduced policy priority for attention and investment with landlords and central government.

In summary:

- **The improvements in estate popularity made in 1980-95 were maintained and there were further gains in 1995-2005.**
- **The popularity gap between the estates and other homes in their local authorities and the nation reduced.**
- **Increased popularity appeared to be partly due to knock-on effects of other changes in the estates (see Sections 8-11), but also due to high housing demand from the knock-on effects of national housing policy and housing market dynamics.**

8. Estate ownership

Since 1980, successive governments have created a diverse set of tools to enable and encourage changes in the ownership and management of council housing in general, and the less popular parts of it in particular. The Right to Buy was the first and best known of these tools, introduced in 1980. Conservative governments in the 1980s also experimented with encouraging councils to transfer whole estates to new ownership and management organisations. Nevertheless, in 1995, all 20 estates were still mainly local authority-owned and managed. An average of only 5% of homes had been sold under the Right to Buy after 14 years of the policy, against a national average of 26%. Four estates had seen a small amount of new building by Registered Social Landlords (RSLs).

However, the period 1995-2005 saw a breakthrough for ownership change in the estates, due to mixed-tenure redevelopment, a Right to Buy breakthrough, and stock transfer.

Mixed-tenure redevelopment

In the period 1988-95, some of the estates saw the demolition of some unpopular or structurally unsound homes, mainly supported by central government funding. One example involved most of the estate (estate 6). From the mid-1990s, a new generation of mixed-tenure redevelopment schemes emerged. By 1995, in one estate a project to replace and improve homes and to include home ownership and RSL renting as well as council renting was being completed (estate 18). Four more estates were due to undergo 'dramatic redevelopments': demolition or tenure change affecting at least a third of homes, with demolition and at least partial rebuilding by RSLs and private developers (estates 11, 12, 13, 15) (Table 4). The following photos show the new kinds of development on the estates.

Table 4: Estates affected by dramatic redevelopment

	Total number of estates	Estate codes
Started before 1995	2	6, 18
Started 1995-2005	4	11, 12, 13, 15
Planned 2005	2	17, 20

Sources: Interviews, 1994, 2005

New education centre developed with New Deal for Communities funding, estate 16

Homes for sale under construction in 2005, estate 12

Homes built for sale in the 1990s, estate 13

Homes built for sale in the 1990s, estate 15

By 2005, these redevelopments, years in the making, had resulted in new mixed-tenure neighbourhoods with new owners and managers, alongside other changes including new design and layout and other regeneration initiatives (Figure 7). Over the past decade, mixed-tenure schemes that involved smaller parts of the estates began in two areas (estates 2, 7). By 2005, there were plans for some redevelopment in one estate and dramatic redevelopment in two more (estates 17, 20).

Figure 7: Tenure mix in estates experiencing redevelopment, 2005

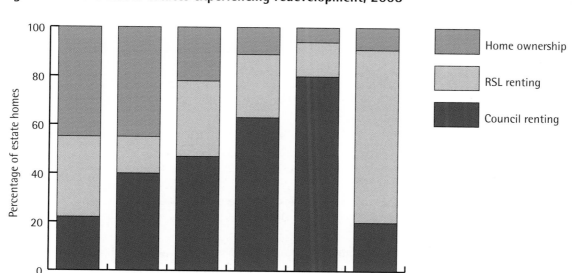

Note: Estate 12 experienced both redevelopment and transfer.
Sources: Interviews, 2005

Dramatic redevelopments were enabled by central government regeneration funding, but they took place because landlords believed that:

- In all cases, previous improvement initiatives in 1980-95 – such as local management, resident involvement and smaller investment – had not overcome poor reputation or unpopularity sustainably or significantly.
- For non-traditionally designed estates, structural or design problems could not be overcome without significant demolition (given existing funding sources or cost-benefit analysis) (estates 6, 11, 12, 17).
- For estates outside London, there was at least sufficient social housing in the estate or wider area (estates 6, 13, 15, 18, 20).
- In all cases, the involvement of RSLs and developers allowed new sources of funding for improving existing homes or building new ones.
- Mixed tenure might be beneficial in itself as a means to overcome problems in unpopular council estates.

All but the first two points encouraged the development of a greater mix of housing tenures in the estates.

Central government policy has directly and indirectly supported more dramatic developments and tenure mixing. The withdrawal of Estate Action, which had provided major capital funding for council estates (including for structural change to non-traditional design) between 1985 and 1995 had an effect. Increasingly, local authorities are being asked to raise their own finance for improvements via transfer and use of assets such as land. Stock transfer, discussed below, prompts the new RSL to plan improvement strategically. Government has also increasingly advocated and supported 'mixed communities' directly.

Some of these estate redevelopments involved substantial substitution of RSL housing for local authority housing, within a total still dominated by social housing. Others involved substantial input of private development.

RSL development on estate land took place in four estates from 1988 to 1994 and further estates saw additional RSL development on estate land or adjacent sites from 1995 to 2005 (for example, estates 3, 7).

The outcomes of mixed-tenure redevelopment are not always predictable, even in terms of tenure itself. In one case, about half of the 200 homes redeveloped for sale had switched to private renting by 2005. Prices fell and owners who wanted to move rented them out, in some estates to avoid negative equity (estate 18).

Other implications of mixed-tenure redevelopment are discussed below, alongside regeneration and investment of all types.

The Right to Buy breakthrough

The take-up of the Right to Buy by estate residents averaged 5% of homes in 1995 but this rate increased in the period 1995-2005 (Figure 8).

There was a particular boom in purchases from 2000 onwards. In 2004/05 for example, one estate saw more homes sold under the Right to Buy than in the previous 24 years of the policy. Another sold one third of the total in that time, and another a quarter. In 1995, the lowest Right to Buy rates among the 20 estates were in estates built in the 1960s and 1970s, mainly made up of flats with non-traditional design and construction. Three per

Figure 8: Tenure mix in estates not affected by redevelopment or stock transfer, 2005

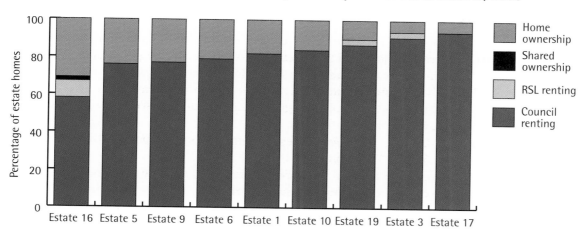

Sources: Interviews with managers, 2005

cent of these homes had typically been sold, in contrast to 6% in the estates of low-rise flats and 5% in the estates comprising houses. But by 2005, Right to Buy had broken into the modern estates. As one manager said: "Right to Buy has accelerated ... we're starting to sell in very difficult areas" (estate 19). Others commented that for the first time ever, sales in their estate were following trends in other parts of the local authority, or were taking place at the same rate. By 2005, sales levels were reaching significant levels in some estates, and, in one, 30% of homes had been sold.

The breakthrough took place because of national and regional factors, as well as changes in the estates themselves:

- The Right to Buy market had matured and it had become easier to get mortgages and insurance even for flats, and buyers were encouraged by the evidence that it was possible to resell and to rent out purchased homes.
- The growth in house prices had encouraged people to buy.
- There was a one-off effect in 2003 when the government announced a reduction in Right to Buy discounts, leading to a rush to beat the deadline.

Local factors were also important in linking the estates to the wider housing market and its trends:

- Improvements and increased popularity had made homes more valuable and more mortgageable. For example, one manager said: "Where there are regeneration schemes, people have bought, as they know they are going to get their money back" (estate 11). All but one of the modern estates here had seen major investment incorporating substantial redesign or demolition just before or over the 1995-2005 period. Some local managers used the increasing rates of Right to Buy purchase as an indicator of increasing popularity. In contrast, in 1995 some had interpreted sales in the same estates as irrational, commenting on, for example, "some very strange purchases" (local manager, 1995, estate 3).
- Only two interviewees mentioned either changes in residents or in their circumstances in explaining increased Right to Buy rates – they referred to higher and more stable incomes (estate 14), and new minority ethnic resident populations with either greater interest in buying, or ability to buy (estate 3).
- Where there were plans for dramatic redevelopment, Right to Buy rates had risen, partly due to the prospect of compulsory purchase prior to redevelopment (estates 17, 20).

This recent boom is likely to slow down due to lower discounts, and may also slow down – or even stop – as house price growth slows. However, it leaves a lasting legacy, as these formerly mono-tenure estates have become linked to the housing market. Their popularity can now be measured over time and in comparison with other areas through prices. One winner from the Right to Buy process – who, notably, had not actually moved and cashed in – told us: "I bought it for £8,700 and now it's worth £100,000. Four beds and a garden, it's lovely" (estate 15).

Tenure change through Right to Buy has implications for estate population (see Section 16). Until initial buyers move (or sublet their properties), the Right to Buy does not mean any change in residents or population mix. Given the late take-up in the 20 estates, in 2005 the biggest effect of Right to Buy policy on these estates was still the indirect impact of much greater sales on other estates, which meant that for 25 years local need for social housing had been ever more concentrated on these estates.

Stock transfer

Three estates have been affected by stock transfer, where local authorities sell or pass on housing to other social landlords (Figure 9).

Figure 9: Tenure mix in estates experiencing stock transfer, 2005

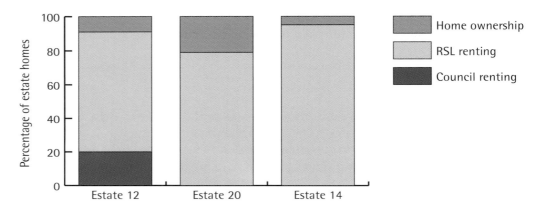

Note: Estate 12 experienced both transfer and redevelopment.
Sources: Interviews, 2005

Stock transfer policy developed incrementally over the 1980s and 1990s. Transfer has been encouraged by central government, and used by local authorities as a pragmatic means to raise funding for improvements, (as new RSL landlords are free of government borrowing restrictions) and to get away from other regulatory restrictions on council landlords. Originally, under previous Conservative governments, it was targeted at unpopular estates, but the policy has widened in scope, and under Labour, it has become mainstream social housing policy aimed at most council housing.

In order for transfer to take place, local authority plans must be approved by central government and by tenants. Two of the 20 estates were in local authorities that transferred their entire stocks (estate 14, 20). Investment was not the only motive, as in both there were histories of tight relationships between councillors and unions, and senior staff saw transfer as the only way to produce significant reforms. Key councillors eventually came to the same view, and tenants were persuaded. In one, the estate's residents' group was the only group to campaign actively against transfer, on the grounds that funding should be available to councils and that RSL tenancy agreements gave residents fewer rights than council tenants, but the view of the majority of the council's tenants prevailed (estate 14). In the third case, the estate was transferred in order to fund dramatic redevelopment, referred to on pages 17-20 (estate 12). Residents were allowed to vote household by household on whether to change landlord, and later individual homes changed hands when residents who voted 'no' moved on. This process followed major tensions in the mid-1990s when some residents took legal action over the way the consultation process was handled, although others later worked very intensively on the process, for example on designs for new homes. As with local authorities, resident support for transfer was largely pragmatic: "When we first heard, we were not sure transfer was going to work. The council didn't have any money to invest but nevertheless they were very secure [and] the rents were low. Quite frankly, most of us signed up to get [new] kitchens" (estate 12).

In one further estate, residents took the initiative on transfer, campaigning through a Tenant Management Organisation (TMO) and a trust they had established for the estate to join an existing housing association (estate 4).

Tenure change through stock transfer has implications for other issues that will be discussed later:

- New management organisations demanded or provided an opportunity for reassessment of management structures and policies (see Section 9).
- Transfer allowed access to funding to improve homes and estates (see Section 10).
- The transfer process meant a tenant consultation effort addressed to individuals and across local authorities, rather than via local groups such as those in the 20 estates (see Section 12).

The estates as mixed-tenure neighbourhoods

In no estate has social housing yet been overtaken by another tenure. However, by 2001 the estates were all to some degree mixed-tenure neighbourhoods. For example, a senior manager said: "There's a reasonable mix of leasehold and tenancies now" (estate 9). By 2005, home ownership accounted for an average of 19% of homes in the estates, four times the 1995 level. Eleven per cent of homes were privately owned through schemes for estate redevelopment and 8% through the mainstream policy of Right to Buy. The proportion of social housing in the 20 estates still placed them in the top twentieth of equivalent sized neighbourhoods nationwide. Nevertheless, as Figure 10 shows, the

Figure 10: Home owners as a proportion of all households

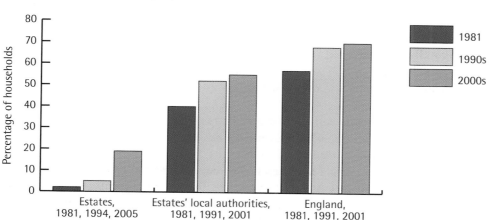

Sources: Interviews, 1982, 1994, 2005; 1981, 1991, 2001 censuses

estates had begun to reduce the gap with home ownership levels in the surrounding local authorities and in England as a whole.

Increased tenure mix has implications for other issues:

- Some housing management staff were concerned about coordination between social landlords and lack of resident access to the smaller landlords (see Section 9).
- Residents and staff felt that the emergence of the private rented sector in the estates had caused management problems and in some cases anti-social behaviour. Residents commented that "you don't know who is responsible, the owners couldn't give two hoots, there is no control over them" (estate 12) and that landlords were "giving houses to any kind of people" (estate 18). Management difficulties in this case pushed the Arm's Length Management Origination (ALMO) responsible for the social housing to become involved in supporting private landlords, offering reference-checking services (see Section 11).

Home originally in council ownership that was redeveloped for sale in 1995 as part of dramatic mixed–tenure redevelopment of the estate, and later rented out privately, estate 18

In summary:

- **The process of tenure mixing seen from 1980 to 1995 accelerated between 1995 and 2005, due to estate redevelopment and the introduction of stock transfer as well as the Right to Buy.**
- **The 'tenure gap' between the level of home ownership in the estates, their local authorities and the nation reduced.**
- **This change was due to mainstream Right to Buy policy, redevelopment targeted on estates, and favourable local and regional housing markets.**

9. Social housing management

Social housing changes seen on the 20 estates included new and increasing numbers of managers, a shift away from local management, and changes in housing management performance. These factors are considered in turn below.

New managers and more managers

Central government attempts to get new organisations to manage council housing have run alongside those for ownership change since the 1980s. From 1980-88, initiatives focused on the organisation of local authority housing departments, and these 20 estates, selected for study as examples of decentralisation, typified that process. Following tenant training and a ballot, local authorities could delegate management to TMOs from 1975, but this option had little impact nationwide and only picked up with funding and central government support from the 1980s. From 1985, local authorities could delegate management to other organisations, but again – without substantial incentives – there was little impact nationwide. From 1995, local authorities were obliged to put management services out to tender under the compulsory competitive tendering (CCT) regime.

Nevertheless, from when these initiatives began up until 1988, local authorities were the main managers of the social housing on all of the estates. By 1995, 18 of the 20 estates were still managed by their local authorities, with one managed by a TMO and one by a private organisation under voluntary competitive tendering (the forerunner to CCT).

Ten years later, the picture was dramatically different (Figure 11). In 2005, only seven of the estates were mainly managed by local authorities:

- Stock transfer has introduced new RSL owner-managers in three estates (estates 12, 14, 20).
- Seven estates were mainly managed by ALMOs, a new type of organisation introduced by government in 2000 as an alternative to stock transfer for councils. ALMOs are 'arm's length management organisations' that are linked to the local authority and manage but do not own housing. After proving resident support and management performance good enough to get an inspection score of two stars out of a possible three from the Housing Inspectorate, local authorities with ALMOs can access new funding for reinvestment in housing without losing ownership estates.

Figure 11: Main social housing manager in the estates

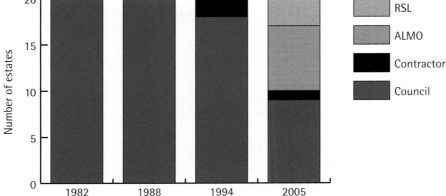

Sources: Interviews, 1982, 1988, 1994, 2005

- Two estates were managed by TMOs, one on behalf of an RSL (estate 14).
- Two were managed by contractors (estates 9, 10).

The principal cause of the change in management was, as with stock transfer, local reaction to central government policy.

Interviewees said that ALMOs were chosen pragmatically in order to release funding for improvements, like stock transfer, and in preference to the transfer option. Where the local authority transferred stock before 2000, senior staff would have preferred the ALMO option if it had been available at the time (estate 14).

The Right to Buy has led to the development of a new category of private renters as well as owner-occupiers in the estates.

In addition, there were now a total of 16 individual RSLs involved as minority landlords and managers across eight estates.

For residents, a change in main management or provider sometimes appeared to be "just a change of name" (residents' group member, estate 19). Sometimes even the name change did not register – for example, a third of residents in one estate where stock transfer took place a year before the 2001 census reported erroneously that they were still council tenants (estate 14). However, the pressures that led local authorities to consider stock transfer and new managers were affecting management organisation and practice in all estates, in tangible ways.

Moving away from local management

This research originated in a study of local housing management, and this model of management persisted in most of these estates through the 1980s and into the 1990s. In most cases, local managers evolved to take on more responsibility, and more homes, and became part of local authority-wide decentralisation. After 1995, and particularly after 2000, there was a rapid move away from 'estate offices' (defined as staffed offices based either in the estate or an adjacent one with public access for the majority of the working week, offering the main housing management services and covering no more than twice as many homes as in the study estate). Estate offices have frequently been replaced by 'area offices' covering larger numbers of homes, or centralised systems (Figure 12).

Figure 12: Estates managed by 'local offices', 1982–2005

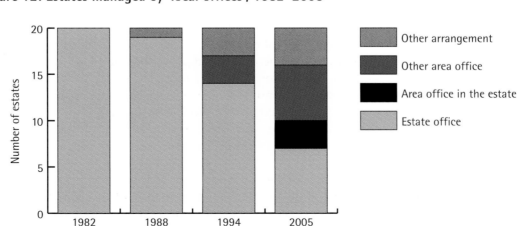

Sources: Interviews, 1982, 1988, 1994, 2005

The number of homes managed by estate and area offices increased steadily through each stage of the research, from about 1,000 homes on average in 1982 to over 2,000 by 2005. Some area offices were responsible for a third of their landlord's stock (for example, estate 13), and one RSL office managed homes in several counties (estate 12). The four estates without estate or area offices were managed from central locations, with limited face-to face-access between staff and residents, for example, through appointments at central offices or staff driving out for meetings with residents (estates 9, 15, 19, 20).

In addition, all the housing management organisations were reorganising to carry out at least some functions centrally. Staff jobs were changing from generic roles in local teams to specialised roles, often in centralised teams. Tenants were being encouraged or required to make contact over the phone or even via the internet. From 1995, the duties carried out within local offices were reduced, which might in itself have progressively reduced the rationale for their continuation. Repairs ordering, chasing and inspection, seen as the most routine tasks, and best suited to management with IT, have been most widely removed from housing officers to central call centres where staff communicate directly with repairs workers or contractors. By 2005, all the management organisations had either set up call centres for handling resident queries or were in the process of doing so. While in 1995 some housing officers complained that chasing arrears dominated their jobs, by 2005, some landlords had also centralised and automated rent accounts. The only functions that bucked this trend were caretaking and tenancy management, which reflected increased powers, activity and expectations on anti-social behaviour.

Decentralised, 'joined-up' housing management with resident involvement has been promoted by the Labour government, which set up a fund to promote 'neighbourhood management' across housing tenures. Despite this, the recentralisation affecting the 20 estates was also largely due to the effects of national policy:

- Senior and local managers attributed changes in management arrangements to the Best Value regime affecting local authorities since 1999. Interviewees in 2005 were less critical of the Best Value regime than interviewees in 1994 had been of its Conservative-originated forerunner CCT, although the demands for restructuring and performance were at least as onerous. Housing staff had become adapted to more competitive environments, and Best Value was linked to investment incentives rather than to potential private sector 'takeovers'. For example, one senior manager said: "Yes, [inspections]'re useful, but not more than every couple of years. They take up so much bloody time…. There are panics, but then there's £200 million [in improvement funding for the ALMO] resting on it" (estate 2).
- Transfers to new managers also precipitated change, as developing business plans for stock transfer and ALMO status demanded re-examination of structures and practice. In this research sample, local authorities were slightly more likely to retain estate and estate-located offices than ALMO and RSL managers.
- According to staff, reorganisation was intended to improve and standardise service quality and to save money, to prepare for ALMOs or to access funds for investment in homes to deliver the Decent Homes Standard by 2010.
- Managers also said they were taking account and advantage of changes in residents' habits and the potential of telephones and IT for transactions. Several senior staff drew analogies between housing and utilities or other mainstream consumer services.

Notably, the two estates managed by TMOs retained estate offices (estates 4, 14). In addition, one estate had won central government funding as part of the neighbourhood management pilot programme. Local housing management there was the base for decentralised efforts across services, and closely linked with a series of other area-based regeneration initiatives such as Sure Start (estate 7; see Figure 17).

Given the reduced roles of housing officers, staffing intensity in the local offices has also reduced. From about 300 homes per officer in 1988 and about 400 in 1995, in 2005 there were 500 homes per officer. The idea of housing officers as generic professionals requiring substantial experience, training and discretion was changing, with a new split between specialised, often centralised staff and more generic customer services staff in local offices and call centres. As one manager said: "The role of the housing officer is much more fragmented, [but] tenants still have the culture where their housing officer is the person who can sort all their problems" (estate 8).

Housing management performance

Despite the emphasis on performance monitoring under the Best Value regime, given the move away from estate offices, it was not possible to obtain all key performance indicators for the estates alone.

Qualitative responses from staff and residents suggested as yet ambiguous effects from changes in management organisation intended to meet the performance indicators and ALMO and transfer business plans:

- Stock transfer and the establishment of ALMOs created opportunities for major reorganisation, although there could be costs to short-term performance. One senior manager admitted that, immediately after stock transfer, "it was utter chaos" (estate 20). Settling down could take a year or more.
- Senior staff, more involved in planning changes and less directly affected by them, tended to be more positive than staff in local offices about the potential performance gains of restructuring, and one senior staff member explicitly argued that reforms could reduce inequalities between different areas: "With a more centralised structure, best practice can be replicated" (estate 11).
- Meanwhile, local and more junior staff were concerned about the effects of reorganisation on more complex cases, and the effect of a lack of personal contact on service quality – and also on their own job satisfaction. According to one staff member: "The council is trying to adopt a supermarket management style to housing, but it can't work ... there's a lot of buck passing" (estate 8). Changes could be painful and confusing for staff: "It feels like we're in a washing machine!" (estate 7).
- While for some estates, a shift to the use of call centres seemed to be working well and filtering simple queries efficiently, for others, there was concern that difficult cases might be lost in the new system and vulnerable users disadvantaged. One local manager said: "[The call centre] has a high turnover and people have no housing experience. It's wasting time" (estate 8). Both senior and local staff felt that at least some residents, at least for the medium term, would not want or be able to use the new telephonic and automated systems. Residents' group members were not enthusiastic about the new systems: "that abomination of a single phone number: 'press one for this, two for that' ..." (estate 12).
- At a certain size or distance, offices may not be able to function as places for face-to-face contact. For example, one resident whose local office was off the estate said: "Not many people bother going there, it doesn't feel like a local housing office" (estate 19).
- As in 1995, most residents' groups felt the local housing office had made a difference to the area: "It's convenient, it's on our doorstep"; "they keep things under control" (estate 16). Among residents interviewed in the street, including in estates that had lost their office, the number of people who felt the housing office had made a difference to the estate was about equal to the number who disagreed. Some who had lost their local office were unhappy: "It was better before when we could talk to them ... now you get passed from person to person" (estate 15); "They're out of touch, there's nobody on our side now" (estate 20). On the other hand, there were also positive

comments: "It's OK because we have a car" (estate 20); and: "The rent is paid through the bank" (estate 17).

If national datasets are used to consider performance, there seems to have been some progress. It is evident, as noted earlier, that the level of empty properties in the estates was below local authority and national averages by 2005 (Figure 5), and overall only six estates had higher proportions empty than their landlords overall, compared with 14 in 1980 and 10 in 1995. Rent collection figures could only be obtained for six estates. Here, managers were collecting an average of 99% of the rent roll, close to local authority and national averages. Other local staff also thought that estate or area arrears targets were being met. These targets were more demanding than performance achieved by estate offices in 1995, which had improved on that of 1988. For example, one area manager said arrears were the lowest they had ever been: "It's a key performance indicator … management systems and IT have improved and there are dedicated income officers" (estate 7).

There were similar problems getting formal performance data on repairs. Here staff opinion was more mixed. Eight local managers thought that the repairs service had improved over the past two years, two thought it had stayed the same, but five thought it had got worse (Figure 13).

Figure 13: Staff and residents' views of changes in repairs services over the past two years[1]

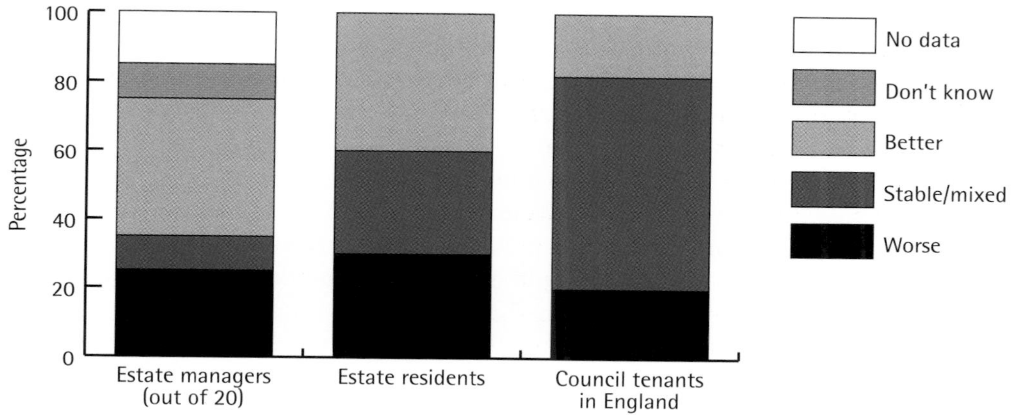

Note: [1] Data obtained in different calendar years
Sources: Interviews with staff, 2005; street interviews in 10 estates, 2005; ODPM, 2005

More significantly, perhaps, many residents praised the repairs service and recent changes. A substantial minority had complaints about slow response, the need to make repeated calls or poor-quality work - "I had a shower fitted and they had to come back eight times" (estate 16) – but, in street interviews, residents were more positive about recent trends than council tenants nationwide (Figure 13). Residents in several areas noted that landlords had reduced their responsibilities over time, particularly for internal repairs. Overall, in only five estates did local managers feel the service was worse than in other estates with the same landlord, or residents' group members, or a majority of street interviewees or housing managers say that the repairs service had got worse over the past two years. In 1980 and 1995, by comparison, 19 and seven of the estates, respectively, had poor repairs services (Table 2).

Figure 14 shows residents' views on environmental problems that housing management was responsible for or can influence. Depending on local structures and on whether estate roads are adopted, housing managers are likely to share responsibility with non-

Figure 14: Residents' attitudes to selected environmental problems in their neighbourhoods

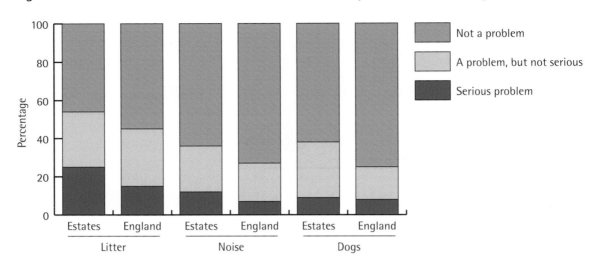

Sources: ODPM, 2005; street interviews in 10 estates, 2005

housing local authority departments covering street cleaning, rubbish collection and environmental health for this issue.

The figure shows that, in 2005, estate residents were more likely to think that litter, noise and dogs were problems than people in England overall, but not by very large margins. Given the extensive estate visits at each stage of this research, continuity in team membership and photographic records, our impression was that overall, the general appearance, cleanliness and maintenance of homes and environments improved from 1980-95. It improved again from 1995-2005, and the gap between these estates and the surrounding areas and country has reduced. None of the estates had the 'neglected, rubbish-strewn environment' seen in all 20 in 1980 and in one, in crisis, in 1995 (Table 2).

Overall, residents' opinions of their landlords were similar to those for social housing overall, and they were more positive than tenants across England about short-term trends. This represents an achievement for estates formerly seen as unpopular and difficult to manage (Figures 15, 16).

Figure 15: Residents' satisfaction with their landlord

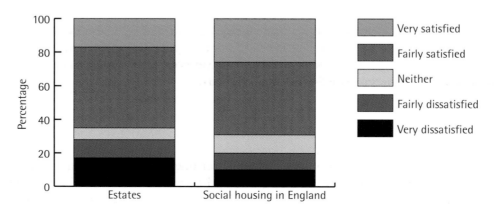

Sources: ODPM, 2005; street interviews in 10 estates, 2005

Figure 16: Residents' views of changes in the service provided by their landlord over the past two years[1]

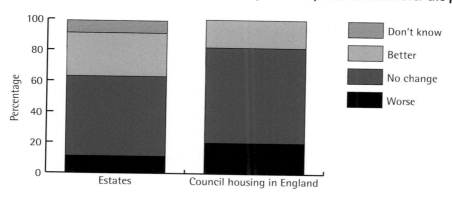

Note: [1] Data obtained in different calendar years
Sources: ODPM, 2005; street interviews in 10 estates, 2005

There was as yet no clear relationship between manager type – council, RSL or ALMO – and performance at estate level or resident satisfaction with the service. There was also no clear relationship between the Audit Commission performance assessment of management performance of entire councils and residents' satisfaction with the landlord for the 20 estates.

In summary, the available evidence suggests:

- **A majority of estates had new managers by 2005 and all had experienced restructuring and new policies, largely due to central government policy as well as landlord-wide responses.**
- **By 2005, most of the estates were managed in similar ways to the rest of the landlords' stocks, with less decentralisation than in the past, representing 'normalisation' of the estates. One manager said that when he arrived in 1995, "the main aim was to get control of the estate, and then to normalise the conditions and practices" (estate 3). Another said: "It's very, very quiet, almost run of the mill" (estate 9).**
- **Housing management performance appeared to improve between 1995 and 2005, and these estates did not stand out from others in their local authority in the way that many did between 1980 and 1995. Resident satisfaction measures were also positive.**
- **In discussion, however, residents and local staff were concerned that efficiency on key performance indicators might be at the price of some aspects of service quality and the needs of some vulnerable residents, and might not be sustainable given recentralisation.**
- **Performance improvement may or may not be due to manager or management changes. Recentralisation may in fact partly be enabled by reduced difficulty of management. Past research has shown that unpopularity and resident deprivation are key drivers of the difficulty and cost of housing management, and have both reduced (see Sections 7 and 16).**

10. Regeneration and investment

There have been several generations of central government area-based regeneration initiatives since 1980 and the 20 estates have formed all or part of the catchment areas for 61 major schemes in all, an average of three each. Thirty-four of these commenced before 1997, and 27 were Labour initiatives (Figure 17).

Figure 17: Estates included in catchment areas for central government area-based regeneration initiatives, 1980–2005

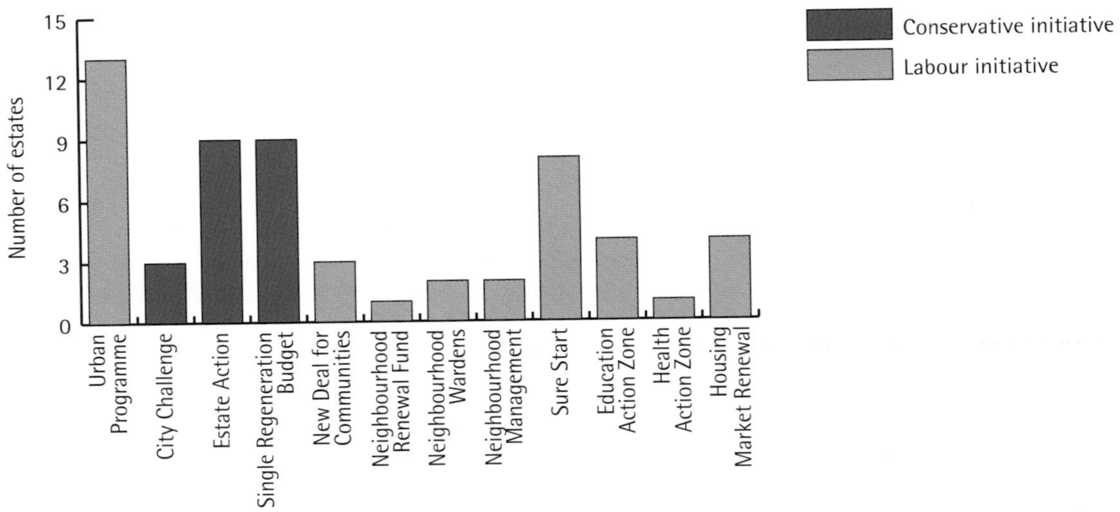

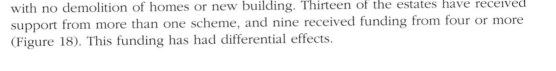

Note: Initiatives listed from left to right from oldest to most recent.
Sources: Staff interviews, 1982, 1988, 1994, 2005

All but three of the estates have received some support from these programmes, including those with dramatic redevelopments (Table 4), minor redevelopment and those with no demolition of homes or new building. Thirteen of the estates have received support from more than one scheme, and nine received funding from four or more (Figure 18). This funding has had differential effects.

Figure 18: Examples of estates in the catchment areas for successive area-based regeneration initiatives, 1980–2005

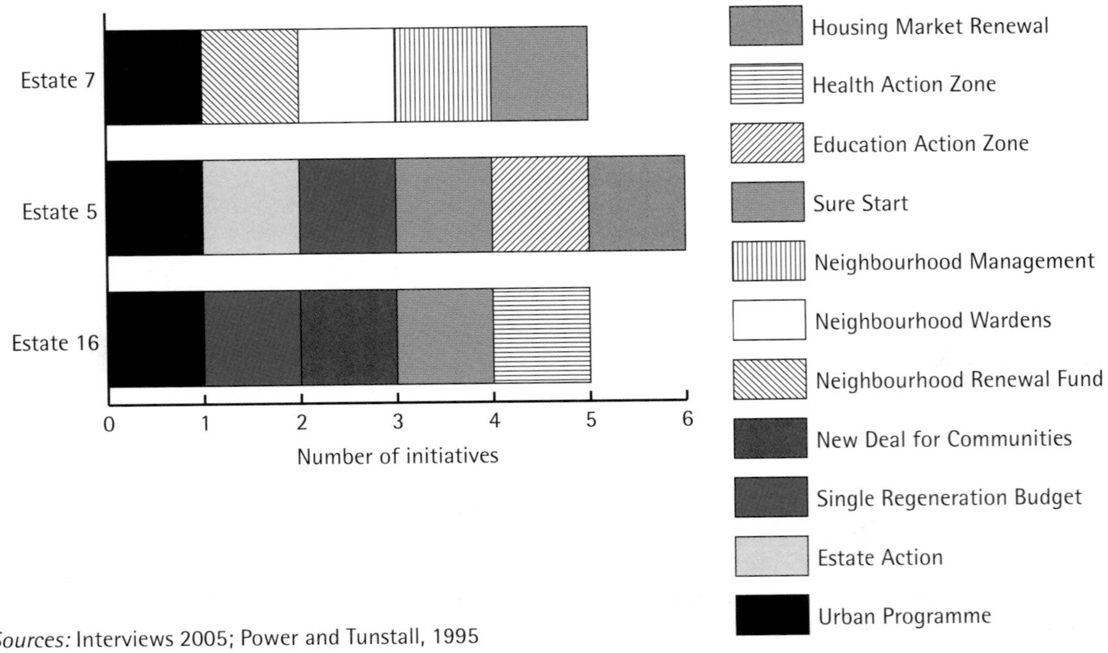

Sources: Interviews 2005; Power and Tunstall, 1995

One of the dramatically redeveloped estates received Estate Action funding in the 1990s. This was used to prevent crime through removing high-level walkways and controlling access to blocks, but failed to deal with the underlying problems (estate 12). The Estate Action improvements were demolished along with the homes when the estates were redeveloped. This money may have been almost entirely wasted in the long term, but there were few similar examples. In general, repeated investment in the same estates through a series of differing projects, while not the most efficient form of long-term strategy, appeared to be of continued benefit.

Before 1997, these programmes were mostly allocated to areas several times larger than the estates, and most involved spending on infrastructure, the environment or economic development. The most important source of funding targeted on housing was Estate Action, which ran between 1985 and 1995 and could allocate very substantial amounts. It supported three of the five dramatic redevelopments. Only one of the estates made up of houses or low-rise blocks of flats received Estate Action funding, and these estates seemed to be overshadowed by other local estates with more serious design and construction problems.

In 1995, a large number of existing regeneration schemes were amalgamated into the Single Regeneration Budget (SRB), which could be spent on physical or social projects, and some estates made up of houses received SRB support.

The post-1997 Labour government has introduced a further range of area-based programmes. Two of the estates that received little before 1995 had major support from this new generation of funding: one was in a New Deal for Communities area, while the other had several new social programmes. A resident in the first estate said: "It was a dump but they're doing it up now" (estate 16). While the New Deal for Communities can provide investment in housing equivalent to a medium-sized Estate Action scheme, some of the other programmes, which concentrate on social development and service improvement, often provide quite small amounts of funding, for example, for short-term provision of extra staff like wardens and neighbourhood managers.

Council homes that were improved and received new extensions as part of dramatic mixed-tenure redevelopment of the estate, estate 13

More estates have also benefited from local authorities' own, if lesser, housing investment funds. Between 1988 and 1995, most estates received investment in basic building fabric through the Housing Investment Programme.

Door-entry system, new porch and bin stores added in the early 1990s using local authority funding, estate 9

Since 1995, local authority housing investment funding has undergone major changes. First, local authorities have been encouraged and enabled to use their own funds to reinvest in their housing. Second, new options have been opened up for local authorities to gain substantial private funding for their homes via transfer and ALMOs. Alongside this, all social landlords are being expected to reach the Decent Homes Standard for all their homes by 2010. A 'decent home' is one that meets the current statutory minimum standard for housing, is in a reasonable state of repair, with reasonably modern facilities and services, and provides a reasonable degree of thermal comfort. By 2005, landlord-wide Decent Home programmes were due to affect almost all the estates, the only exceptions being those that have recently undergone dramatic redevelopment. Two more of the four estates that tried and failed to get Estate Action were due to receive support released via stock transfer (estate 14) and ALMO status (estate 19).

The Decent Homes policy requires local authorities to take a strategic approach and to plan long-term investment needs and funding sources across all their estates, ending incrementalism and enabling economies of scale. The standard also creates another pressure for centralisation within housing organisations, as within housing management. By reintroducing a planned approach to maintenance, it also blurs the divide between repairs and capital and regeneration work.

Despite the fact that the great majority of the 20 estates had not yet received any investment benefit from stock transfer, ALMOs or the Decent Homes process, staff and some residents' groups were excited about plans for investment. However, most local managers and residents' group members criticised the Decent Homes Standard and its enforcement as too low level, narrowly focused on homes rather than the environment, inflexible, and as providing perverse incentives. For example, one maintenance manager said: "You could just repair the electrics – that's an easy job and might make properties compliant but most tenants might not spot the changes" (estate 7). Another pointed out that there was no element covering lifts (estate 9). In fact, almost all the landlords had developed their own local, higher standard. Residents complained that strategy was being based on sketchy stock condition surveys, or that they could not understand how priorities were being decided.

In addition to central and local government sources, four estates have effectively provided their own funding for redevelopment and improvement, through land sales, and in five more areas there were plans to do this. For example, in one case, the sale of land for a new supermarket provided the main funding for a major estate redevelopment, although SRB funding provided training and employment assistance to residents and a Health Action Zone supported projects there. Five more planned to use this process.

Supermarket built on the site of demolished estate homes. Land sold to fund estate's dramatic redevelopment of the rest of the site, estate 12

Fundraising through realising public assets is imaginative, but can only be done once, and does not work as well outside high-value housing markets. Densification may not be successful or achievable even where values are high. For example, one resident said, "They're thinking of building on the green, we want to stop that, we've got enough houses" (estate 15).

The effects of investment

The effects of redevelopment on tenure mix were covered in Section 8, but there were also significant physical effects. Two redevelopment schemes were so extensive that estates changed from comprising mainly medium-rise, non-traditional flats (see Table 1) to mainly houses (estate 15), and to a mixture of houses and low-rise traditional flats, forming an unrecognisable neighbourhood (estate 12). New homes looked attractive and transformed the appearance of some estates. In most cases, residents were pleased with the new homes created after redevelopment. For example, one said: "It looks much better, like a normal house" (estate 18). Overall, just one estate where redevelopment was planned still had structural and design problems in 2005, compared with six in 1995 (Table 5).

Of the six completed dramatic redevelopment schemes, four were judged by staff and residents to have been very successful (estates 6, 12, 13, 15). In the fifth, conditions had improved, although residents and staff were still concerned about crime in 2005 (estate 11). Some residents of redeveloped estates felt the physical, tenure and atmospheric transformation was so great that their area could no longer be called an 'estate'. A senior housing officer in one redeveloped area reported that even though residents rejected the idea of renaming the area, children living there now describe their home with the name for the wider local neighbourhood, and not the former name for the estate (estate 12). However, residents reported some drawbacks. For example, one said: "The design of the new build is atrocious ... we've lost a third of the space" (estate 15). Residents of new homes also reported that their outgoings were higher because of having to pay higher RSL rents or water rates that had previously been included in rent.

In the sixth scheme, the estate was completely redeveloped, but it was designated as having an uncertain future in 1995. After 10 years of hard work by residents, local managers and further investment, its future was no surer in 2005 (estate 18). There were still considerable problems of low demand, poor reputation and anti-social behaviour. Empty homes were being demolished piecemeal, and staff were expecting the housing market renewal pathfinder, a central government-funded organisation working with two local authorities, to propose more significant demolition in the area.

In 2005, there were plans for redevelopment in two further estates, including the final modern estate, where residents thought conditions had worsened 1995-2005 (estates 17, 20). Landlords had stopped letting homes in both estates and residents complained about empty properties and uncertainty. In the London estate, one resident said: "Because people know it's being knocked down, they don't look after it, the people and the housing officers ..." (estate 17). In the other estate, a resident said: "There was a community here. Now there's all the empty houses ... we've got no neighbours" (estate 20). However, earlier interviews at estates with redevelopments judged successful by staff and residents in 2005 might have produced similar results.

In addition to the changes outlined here, other implications of these redevelopments include the creation of mixed-tenure neighbourhoods (see Section 8), a reduction in social rented homes, increased ease of management (see Section 9) and population movement (see Section 10).

Outside the dramatically redeveloped estates, there were smaller redevelopments in some estates (Table 4) and investment in homes and estates, including security measures, re-roofing, new heating systems and new kitchens and bathrooms, as well as improvements to estate environments, including demolition of raised decks, new or improved parks, better fencing, new play equipment, traffic calming and new car-parking places.

Estate residents prioritised improvements in the amount and quality of housing and the quality of the environment more than residents of England overall. However, they had similar views on their own homes to other social housing residents nationwide, and were only slightly less satisfied than those nationwide (Figure 19 – the 10 estates include those affected by dramatic redevelopment as well as those not affected). This is a considerable achievement for the estates, given that they include a higher proportion of features associated with lower satisfaction, such as urban locations and flats rather than houses.

Figure 19: Residents' satisfaction with their homes

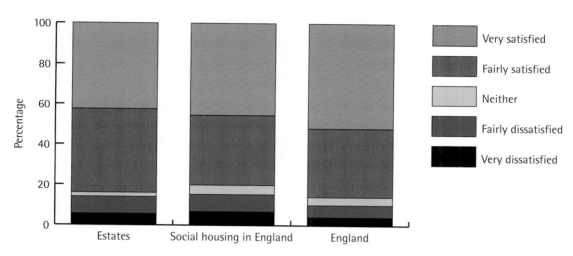

Sources: ODPM, 2005; street interviews in 10 estates, 2005

Regeneration and investment have had effects on resident and manager assessments of their estates (Section 6) as well as the estates' popularity (Section 7), tenure mix (Section 8) and the management problems they pose (Section 9). They also have potential knock-on effects on crime and resident activity (Section 12), as lobbying for, and being consulted on the implementation of regeneration and investment were a major focus for resident groups' activity.

In summary:

- **The pattern of successive and mostly successful bouts of regeneration and investment seen in 1980-95 continued in 1995-2005.**
- **The most dramatic effects came from dramatic estate redevelopment, although this could not succeed in all market conditions.**
- **The worst physical and design problems in the estates had been addressed.**
- **Investment was in transition from programmes targeted on less popular estates to a more strategic approach across whole council and RSL stocks.**

11. Crime and anti-social behaviour

In 19 of the 20 estates, high levels of crime and vandalism were among the factors that led to estate-based management initiatives at the start of the 1980s (Table 2). In 1995, crime remained a major or even greater concern for residents and managers than previously, partly reflecting the nationwide rise in victimisation over the period 1981-95. In 1995, no residents' group thought that crime was 'not a problem'.

Ten years later, some residents' groups and a third of residents interviewed on the street felt that crime was no longer a problem, although there was still a gap between the estates and other social housing and the nation overall (Figure 20).

Figure 20: Residents' views of the severity of the crime problem in their area

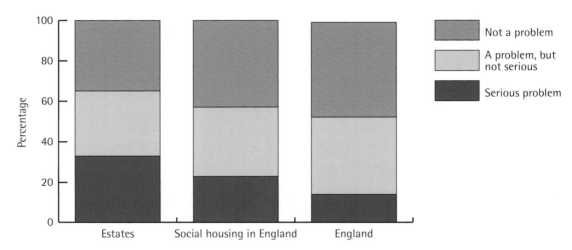

Sources: ODPM, 2005; street interviews in 10 estates, 2005

When residents' groups were asked what was bad about living in the estates, in 1995, about half mentioned crime and fear of crime, whereas by 2005, only a small minority of group members and a quarter of people interviewed in the street referred to this. In one estate, a group member said: "It has reduced dramatically" (estate 3); elsewhere, another said: "Crime is not a big issue, not compared to what it was 10 years ago" (estate 14), and in a third case, it was reported that "the police and authorities are on top of crime and vandalism now" (estate 5). The vast majority of managers also felt that crime had reduced between 1995 and 2005. In one redeveloped estate, a senior manager noted that some residents wanted a CCTV system, but that crime levels were too low to warrant it (estate 12).

Residents still mentioned crimes including burglary, robbery, shootings, drug dealing and use, vandalism, joyriding and arson that had occurred in the estates or affected people they knew. Concern about crime had not gone away but appeared to be less pressing. Some were concerned to point out that the situation was 'normal': "It's like anywhere, isn't it?" (estate 14). Overall, we judged that four estates had high levels of crime and vandalism, compared with 19 in 1980 and seven in 1995 (Table 2).

Both national social trends and estate factors appear to be behind the changes:

• National figures for victimisation from the British Crime Survey (Dodd et al, 2004) fell continuously and significantly and by 2004/05 crime levels were close to 1981 levels again. The proportion of people in England who thought that crime was a problem in their area fell from 73% in 1994/95 to 55% eight years later, according to the Survey of English Housing (ODPM, 2004; DCLG, unpublished, table S709). Estate residents appear to have benefited from this trend, although it is not possible to say if concern about crime was falling faster or slower in the estates than in the national or police areas in which they are located.

• Regeneration or redevelopment had resolved long-running design problems such as dark, empty car parks and walkways, and hiding places. In one area, redevelopment successfully resolved a state of crisis associated with violent disorder, through the demolition of empty homes on the estate, demolition of the only one-bedroom accommodation in the estate which had been mainly inhabited by young single people including some connected with crime, and improved security in existing homes (estate 13). However, in another estate, redevelopment had not resolved crime problems, and nine out of the 10 street interviewees said that crime was a serious problem, as did managers (estate 11). Interviews took place shortly after a shooting in the estate, but residents and staff also reported ongoing problems of violence, muggings and motorbike riding.

- A total of seven estates had CCTV systems, including all the non-traditionally designed estates, but also two made up of houses where the system viewed not block entrances but public streets (estates 16, 20). In all cases, staff and residents felt that CCTV was having a positive effect either on crime rates or fear of crime, even if there were problems such as unobserved areas, poor images or court reluctance to act on pictures alone.

- Residents in two areas mentioned more policing and the introduction of Police Community Support Officers to supplement the force as beneficial factors (for example, estate 16).

One residents' group member said that crime had not been reduced but instead, "it's changed type. There's more graffiti and anti-social behaviour" (estate 19). Others said: "The problem is more with kids now and petty vandalism" (estate 3).

In considering this issue, as with crime, estate residents were more concerned by a range of anti-social behaviours than residents of England as a whole, and the gaps for vandalism, graffiti and harassment were greater than for crime (Figure 21). In combination, 'crime and vandalism' topped the list when residents were asked which three things they wanted improved in their areas; 43% of interviewees cited this issue, compared with 32% nationwide (Figure 25).

Figure 21: Residents' views of the severity of selected anti-social behaviour problems in the estates, 2005 and in England, 2003/04

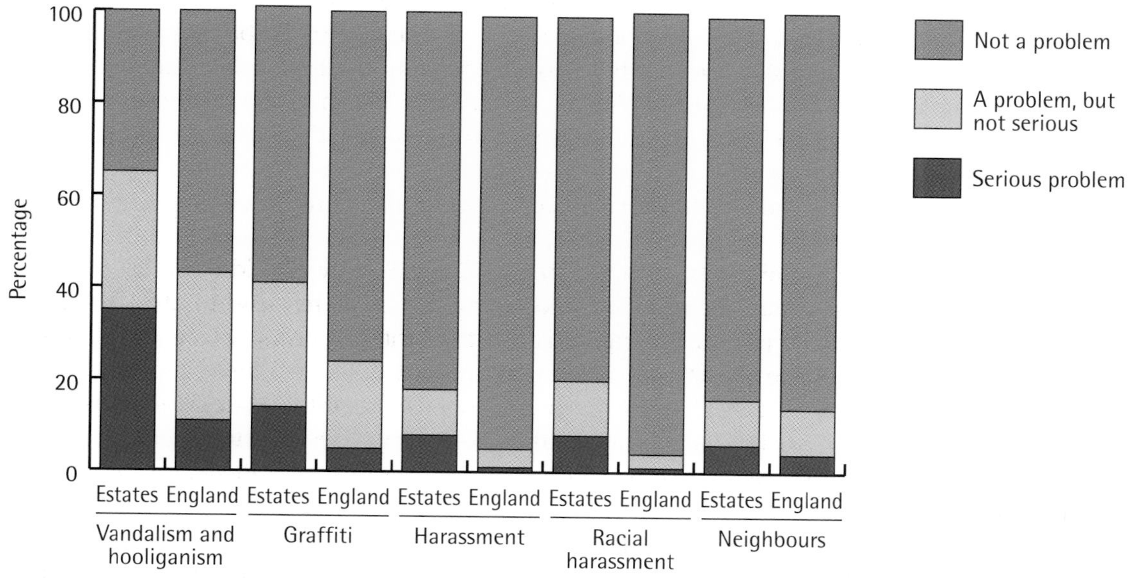

Sources: ODPM, 2005; street interviews in 10 estates

Reliable information to compare anti-social behaviour in estates and elsewhere was not available, although one estate accounted for a quarter and another nearly a fifth of all Anti-Social Behaviour Orders (ASBOs) granted to their local authorities.

Although residents mostly felt harassment was not a serious problem (Figure 21), they described incidents such as "a couple of old blokes who like a drink who get taunted" (estate 15), "little ASBO kids … they bully one-parent families … they don't mess with me. I've got two big sons" (estate 17).

Racial harassment incidents of different sorts were described in estates with small minority ethnic popularities and 'majority minority' ones. Residents in one estate with a large minority population said: "Somali gangs on our side, our silly white gangs and the black gangs, it's just the kids"; "My boys had it, 36 kids [in class], only two white boys" (estate 17). In an estate that was 95% white, a resident who had come as an asylum seeker from Eritrea said: "I was egged when I moved onto the estate but I couldn't say anything bad about it now". Twenty per cent of residents in street interviews in both high and low minority population estates thought that racial harassment was a problem, four times the figure for England overall (Figure 21).

Connected to concern about anti-social behaviour was a strong feeling that more needed to be done for young people in the estates. The second most frequent item on the wish list was 'facilities for young people', mentioned by 36% of residents, similar to the nationwide figure of 39% (Figure 25).

In the only estate where both residents and staff felt conditions had got worse over the last 10 years of the study period, graffiti, vandalism (such as kids kicking down fences) and anti-social behaviour (such as drug use and "putting wires across roads to catch cars", as one resident described it), were felt to discount all the benefits of the reduction in crime, and were the biggest problem for the estate (estate 19). In another estate with an uncertain future in 2005, anti-social behaviour was seen as one of the main negative things about the estate, and involved underage drinking, motorbike riding, name calling, and youths hanging around in groups of up to 40, which residents found intimidating (estate 18).

In 1995, the term 'anti-social behaviour' was not in widespread usage, but managers and residents were nevertheless concerned about activities such as joyriding, intimidation, drug use, harassment, nuisance and loitering. Staff and residents found it difficult to judge whether levels of anti-social behaviour had actually increased since 1995, or whether its salience had increased as crime reduced. There are no robust measures to assess this in other ways.

In general, residents and staff felt that measures taken by landlords to reduce anti-social behaviour were having some effect. As part of management reorganisation, landlords had developed new procedures and specialised teams to handle difficult cases and prepare legal evidence. They had tightened definitions in tenancy agreements and increased enforcement efforts. All the 18 local authorities in which the estates are located had, like almost all authorities nationwide, applied for and issued ASBOs after they became available in 1999. ASBOs had been taken out against residents or to prevent people entering the estate in six of the 20 estates, and in three others landlords had used the non-legally binding Acceptable Behaviour Contract (ABC) model instead. ASBOs and ABCs were only a small part of activity and were used as a last resort, and some residents queried their value for money, but in most cases residents felt they had been effective (estate 5).

In summary:

- **The crime problem in the estates that persisted from 1980 to 1995 appears to have reduced significantly by 2005, and is part of the reason for the reduction in the numbers of estates in decline or crisis.**
- **The reduction in crime appears to mirror the national trend, although estate improvements and management may have helped these estates benefit from the trend.**
- **Concerns about anti-social behaviour are important, however, and may be partly due to a rise in incidents but also due to the decrease in crime.**

12. Residents' groups

Given the extent of changes in estate ownership, management organisation and staffing over the 25 years since 1980, the consistency of resident activity in the estates, of individual organisations and even individual activists, was remarkable. For example, three groups active in 2005 had been started as part of the original initiatives in the estates at least 25 years ago, although there had been periods when the groups were less active or inactive (estates 5, 8, 19). About half of the group members interviewed in 2005 who gave figures had been involved in their group for over five years, and individuals in four estates had been involved for over 10 years. In contrast, only seven estates were still managed by the same organisation as in 1995, and only one local manager had been working in the same area for 10 years – in fact most had less than three years' knowledge of the area.

However, the number of active, landlord-recognised groups in the estates with an interest in housing management and the overall welfare of the estates as places, such as tenants' and residents' associations or TMOs, reduced between 1995 and 2005. In 1995, 16 of the estates had active residents' groups with involvement in housing issues and other community activity, which had been a very important element of progress in the estates. No estate gained a residents' group between 1995 and 2005, while four estates lost groups. Among the existing groups, one went from being a TMO in development to a TMO in action, a new management organisation, as noted earlier, with financial and managerial responsibility (estate 14), but overall the level of activity appears to have reduced. Of the 14 active groups, four had very few members in 2005, were not able to contribute significantly to interaction with management or their own projects, and faced an uncertain future, so overall the number of estates with little resident involvement increased from seven in 1995 (Table 1) to 10 in 2005.

Estate-level factors – estate improvement – appeared to be the main cause of this slight reduction in active residents' groups:

- Of the four estates that lost groups over the period, in three cases the loss followed substantial estate redevelopment, which left the estates improved (estates 12, 13, 15). In one case, the handful of members noted: "There was massive interest in meetings with Estate Action, but it dies down" (estate 15).
- In the fourth estate, a TMO group shrank over time, and by 2005 it had been suspended following allegations of mismanagement of funds (estate 20).

The estates that had residents' groups in both 1995 and 2005 were varied, and having a group did not guarantee continued improvements throughout the period. However, in several estates, residents' groups had been at least part of the explanation for significant changes in estates since 1995. One entrepreneurial group had developed a TMO, a community trust, community businesses and services including a nursery, and was campaigning for stock transfer to raise investment finding (estate 4). In another estate, residents had developed a TMO and used it to restore an estate office and housing officer that had been removed in the early 1990s, and to extend the service with an estate-based handyman (estate 14). This was in spite of a lengthy stock transfer process that had placed the future of tenant management in doubt. Another group had helped to win neighbourhood management and regeneration funding for the estate (estate 7). In two other estates, residents had significant involvement in major redevelopment plans contributing to the local controversy that meant it was not possible to speak to staff in one estate (estate 17), and challenging New Deal for Communities proposals for densification and the influx of homes for sale in another (estate 10).

Other residents' groups mentioned smaller initiatives: successful campaigns on minor environmental problems, with clean-up days (estate 16); ongoing discussions on creating new play areas (estate 5); and as yet unsuccessful ones on drink and drug use, traffic calming and in-curtilage parking (estate 19). A minority of residents' groups also ran regular activities in the estates, such as an after-school club, savings club, keep-fit classes and a youth club. Groups with a concern for housing issues are usually a minority of all community groups with an interest in a local area.

Where there was no active group, residents and staff often said that they needed one to help and sustain improvements or were trying to establish groups, although notably, only one of the estates had a local office to make this convenient for staff. Residents also said that it could be more difficult to organise residents in multi-social landlord estates, as each landlord encouraged their own.

When asked how much account landlords took of tenants' views, there were varied responses, but there were similar complaints to those from several groups in 1995: "If they have an agenda, they're going to go ahead regardless" (estate 7); "They don't listen" (estate 19). Landlords were supplying similar sorts of support for tenant involvement as they did in 1995. Almost all groups had access to a meeting space for free, and most also had access to free photocopying. More had access to opportunities for training than in 1995, but the training tended to be provided centrally by the landlord and most groups had not taken advantage of it. A minority of groups appeared to have regular contact with a support worker – a community development worker, or a tenant participation worker. Funding for groups again varied between nothing, one-off grants, self-raised funding and annual sums.

Yet by 2004, the salience of tenant participation through estate-based groups appeared to have declined somewhat for local housing managers. When asked about overall trends in the estates since 1995, two managers mentioned improved staff–tenant relations (estate 3, 14), and one referred to higher expectations on the part of residents (estate 12). However, there was very little mention of resident involvement in housing management, regeneration or other decision making to explain trends since 1995. Again, this contrasts with the position in 1995, where although managers identified problems including low numbers involved, unrepresentativeness and conflicts between rival groups, local managers considered resident involvement one of the main factors in improvement, alongside capital expenditure and local management.

All local authorities have been required to demonstrate tenant involvement over new national policy areas since 1997; assessing tenant satisfaction has become a key performance indicator for landlords under Best Value, and 10 had had to consult and canvas tenants collectively over stock transfer and ALMO status. However, members of resident groups in these estates – and the local staff – appeared to have had little involvement in these landlord-wide processes. Most residents' groups said that they had not been involved in consultation over Best Value. Two groups mentioned involvement in stock transfer, where it had taken place (estate 12, 14), although in one group, the chair had been actively opposed to transfer. In an area where an ALMO had been set up, members of the group that had been established in the estate for 25 years said that they had not been involved (estate 19). No group from the 20 estates had members as tenant representatives on RSL or ALMO boards, although some groups explicitly chose not to take part in what was available, for example, seeing tenant RSL board members as having given up their independence (estate 14). It is possible that Decent Homes work may boost groups and consultation. Groups in four areas had been consulted on implementation (estates 3, 7, 12, 19). As one resident group member put it: "The real test will be major works happening next year" (estate 19).

Lower levels of activity and lower profiles for residents' groups from the 20 estates could be interpreted as part of the 'normalisation' process identified above. However, they appear to be at least partly associated with a shift in consultation away from not just these 20 estates but from estate-level to landlord-wide topics and fora. Some local staff reported that they did not have responsibility for tenant consultation, which was now carried out by central specialised staff. For staff, tenant participation seemed to be overshadowed by management reorganisation and new issues such as anti-social behaviour, and had been made less easy given the reduction in estate-based offices.

In summary:

- **The number of active residents' groups in estates declined between 1995 and 2005, and the salience of participation to housing managers and residents also appears to have declined slightly.**
- **This appears to be due largely to estate improvement, particularly through redevelopment, but has also been affected by changing priorities in the national and local policy agenda.**

13. Facilities and activities

More than half of the estates were described at the start of the estate-based management initiatives as having an isolated location with few shops and social facilities (Table 2). This pattern has not changed. In fact, since 1995, facilities in the estates appear to have followed the nationwide trend of loss of local branches for major public and private facilities and small independently run shops to greater centralisation. Residents on one estate mentioned the forthcoming loss of a local laundrette as part of estate redevelopment, and the loss of a doctor's surgery and a post office. In another case, a mainstream bus service had been cancelled and was now funded by time-limited Sure Start and neighbourhood management money. One resident said: "It seems like everything is going" (estate 18); another that "the nearest post office is three miles away, we need new shops not other buildings" (estate 16). Residents complained about the cost and quality of some local shops: a very expensive corner shop, a crowded local supermarket and post office, and a chemist with limited opening hours. However, residents saw shopping facilities as less of a priority for improvement than did people nationwide (Figure 25) and after family and friends, 'good location' and 'nearby amenities' were the most-quoted positive things about the areas in street interviews.

Most residents' groups mentioned that their estate had some kind of activity for small children and older young people, including play spaces, Sure Start and a new nursery, regular youth clubs – some resident-run – and other activities and play spaces. One resident said: "There's loads of different things" (estate 16). However, commonly, residents felt that providing more facilities and services for young people was a priority for the area, although slightly less than the national average (Figure 25). Residents in a minority of groups mentioned some regular activities for older people, as well as annual events like a Christmas lunch. The number of community groups and regular activities was much greater in the London estates, linked to ethnic diversity and groups related to cultural and religious activities.

The majority of estates had some space available for communal activities, ranging from small rooms that could be booked for free, to large, purpose-built, staffed centres with a range of subsidised and market hire rates. Several estates had received new or improved community centres since 1995, but while some had busy schedules of local voluntary activity and mainstream local authority leisure provision, two residents' groups mentioned underused community buildings as a problem, and one bemoaned the lack of revenue funding to support activities there: "We've got beautiful buildings. But now we need provision for the community" (estate 3).

In summary:

- **There was a slight decline in private and public facilities available in estates between 1995 and 2005, which appears to reflect national trends, although in a few areas regeneration initiatives were reproviding or adding services.**
- **Many estates were still relatively well off for community facilities and activities, but these relied on revenue funding and volunteer effort, which was not available everywhere and might not be sustained.**

14. Estate-linked schools

In 1995 and 2005, estate-linked schools – schools that managers or residents' groups reported that estate children aged 11-16 were most likely to attend – were identified (see Appendix for details). In both 1995 and 2005, results at GCSE and 'A' level for these schools lagged behind those of their local education authorities (LEAs) as a whole and for England, while absence rates were higher. However, since 1995, the gaps on GCSE results and absence between the estate-linked schools, their LEAs and England have dramatically narrowed. This suggests a significant reduction in inequality (Figures 22, 23), although estate-resident children do not necessarily make up a majority of the roll at estate-linked schools, and the schools identified did not all educate the majority of children from the estates.

Figure 22: GCSE results, 1994 and 2004

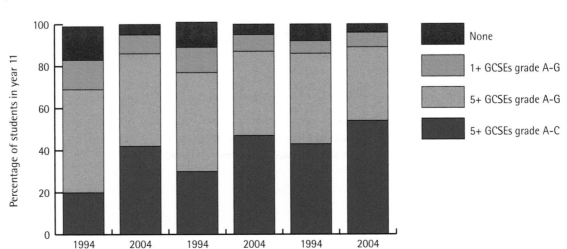

Source: Power and Tunstall, 2005

Figure 23: Absence from secondary schools, 1994 and 2004

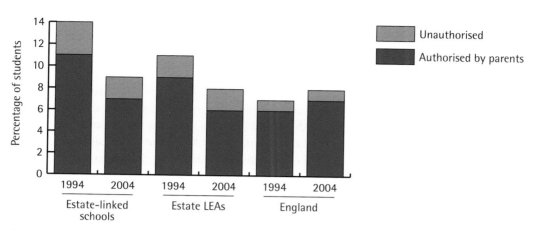

Source: Power and Tunstall, 2005

A good school was mentioned by a resident as an asset of an area otherwise seen as in decline (estate 19). However, more residents expressed dissatisfaction than contentment. Despite the improvements, 18% of estate residents selected schools and colleges as priorities for improvement, compared with only 10% of respondents across England, according to the Survey of English Housing (Figure 25). Residents interviewed in the street also mentioned poor schools among the negative things about the area in four estates. One resident, who was a school governor, said local schools were excluding too many pupils and were "breeding new criminals" (estate 8), and another said that "the quality of the local school is awful, we had to fight to go elsewhere" (estate 17).

Estate children did not necessarily make up a majority of the students at estate-linked secondary schools, in either 1994 or 2004, but there was no evidence to suggest that schools had improved their results by avoiding admitting estate children. Residents in one area said that the good secondary school was hard to get into, and in another area, a resident commented that "schools look down" on the estate and its children (estate 18), but these were ongoing problems. Thirty-eight per cent of children at estate-linked secondary schools were eligible for free school meals in 2005, suggesting similar benefit claimant rates to estate households, and compared with 14% in England.

Four estates were within Education Action Zones (Figure 17), recognising particular needs, but this had not affected the estate-linked school in all cases, and GCSE results in these areas in 2005 did not appear different from other estates (estates 4, 13, 17, 18).

In summary:

- **There were significant improvements in educational performance and attendance at estate-linked secondary schools between 1994 and 2004, although there is evidence that residents are not satisfied with schools.**
- **The causes of this are unclear, but improvements do not seem to be due to schools avoiding enrolling estate children.**

15. Residents' satisfaction with their areas

Residents' satisfaction with their local areas sums up a wide range of issues, likely to include all those considered above: the management and condition of public and semi-public spaces, as well as crime levels, and facilities and activities.

Overall, residents were less likely to be very satisfied with their area than those in social housing and England overall, but were more likely than residents of social housing generally to be very or fairly satisfied (Figure 24). In the one estate where a majority of people in street interviews were very dissatisfied, nine out of the 10 people interviewed there said that crime was a serious problem, as did managers (estate 11).

Figure 24: Residents' satisfaction with their area

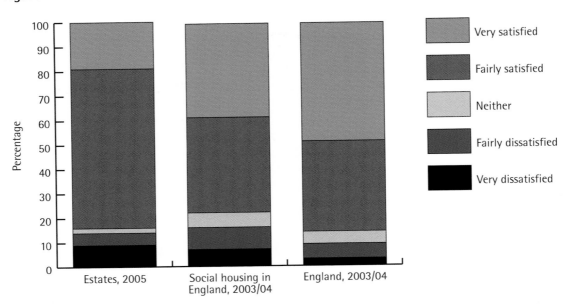

Sources: ODPM, 2005; street interviews in 10 estates, 2005

When residents were asked what the best things were about the area, like residents in other studies and areas, the vast majority of residents mentioned family, friends and community spirit first: "I like it, it's the people" (estate 7).

When asked what things needed improvement in their areas, estate residents were more likely to have suggestions than residents nationwide (Figure 25). Despite evidence of progress and reduction of gaps between estates, their local authorities and the nation from 1980 to 2005, residents were still more likely to be concerned about the major policy areas of crime and vandalism, housing and the environment than residents of England as a whole.

Figure 25: What residents wanted to see improved in their areas

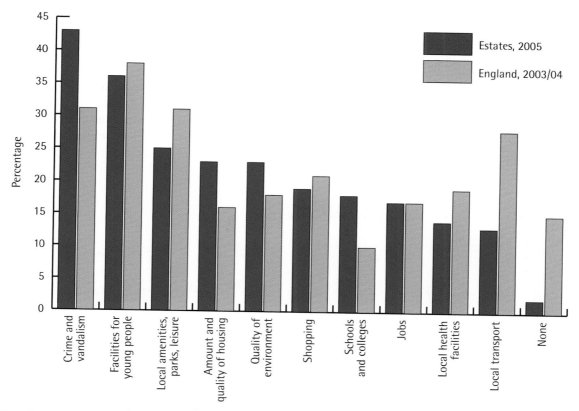

Note: Respondents could select three priorities.
Sources: ODPM, 2005; street interviews in 10 estates, 2005

In summary:

- **By 2005, residents' satisfaction with their areas was comparable to residents of social housing nationwide; improvements in popularity, physical conditions and housing management, as well as reduced crime, are likely to have contributed to this.**
- **Like other residents nationwide, estate residents were most concerned about crime and vandalism and facilities for young people.**

16. Estate populations

So far, we have examined changes in the estates as places. The following section looks at changes in the characteristics of estate populations.

Snapshots of resident characteristics can change over time for one or both of the following reasons:

- Changes in the characteristics of individual residents and households through, for example, ageing, illness, or employment.
- Changes in the mixture of individuals and households, as people move in and out of the estates.

Changes in the estates as places, discussed earlier, could affect both these processes. In addition, changes in estate populations could have knock-on effects for the estates as places. Changes in population could be due to changes in the characteristics of the national or regional population, or in the processes that determine how people come to live in different areas, including, for example, estate popularity relative to other options, landlord allocations policies and overall demand for social housing.

The starkest finding for the period 1980-95 was how the estate populations had become increasingly polarised from those of their surrounding local authorities and from the national averages between the 1981 and 1991 censuses in terms of residents' economic status, age mix and household types. Have these trends continued? The following sections consider this question in terms of employment and economic activity, age and household profiles, resident ethnicity and health issues, before considering how far the changes on the estates can be said to reflect changes in the circumstances of individuals already on the estates or changes in the mix of individuals living on the estates.

Less unemployment and more employment

Unemployment rates for estate residents were dramatically lower in 2001 than in 1991 (Figure 26).

Figure 26: Unemployed residents as a percentage of economically active residents aged 16–74

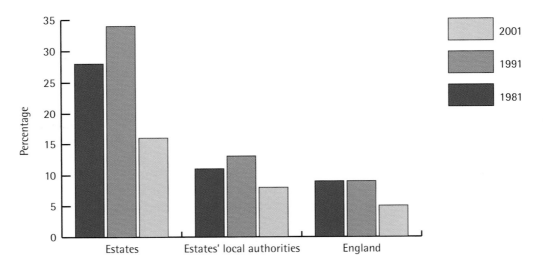

Sources: 1981, 1991, 2001 censuses

In 1991, on average across the estates, 34% of all economically active people aged 16-74 were unemployed, but by 2001 the figure was only 15%. Every single estate saw drops in the unemployment rate, and in two the rate fell by more than 25 percentage points (estates 13, 20). Unemployment also fell for estates' local authorities and England overall, but less sharply, which meant a dramatic convergence between levels of unemployment in the estates and their local authorities and the nation as a whole.

Employment rates for estate residents were also dramatically higher in 2001 than 1991 (Figure 27). In 1991, on average, only 36% of 16- to 74-year-olds on the estates were employed, while by 2001 the figure was 47%. There was some variation; the employment rate ranged from 29% (estate 15) to 61% (estate 14) across the estates. On average, three quarters of employed residents were working full time, with a quarter working part time.

Figure 27: Employed residents as a percentage of those aged 16–74

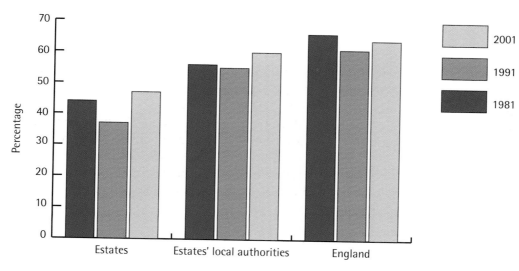

Sources: 1981, 1991, 2001 censuses

The overall employment trends were positive. One RSL housing manager noted: "The estate had really high unemployment; a lot are now working" (estate 7), and a senior RSL officer said: "Our customers have more money, they feel better, it is possible to lift people out of poverty" (estate 14). Just 17% of residents in street interviews identified jobs as one of the top three things to improve in the area, no higher than for all residents in England (Figure 25).

However, part of the drop in unemployment appears to be explained by an increase in the number of economically inactive residents: those outside the labour market who were neither working nor looking for work, including those who had retired, were disabled, studying or caring for friends or relatives (Figure 28).

Figure 28: Economically inactive residents as a percentage of those aged 16–74

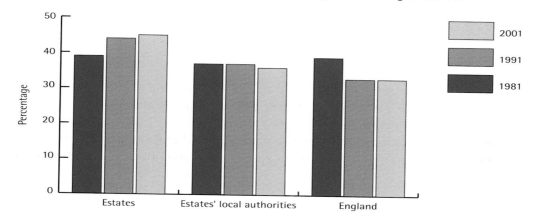

Sources: 1981, 1991, 2001 censuses

By 2001, the profile of the residents of the 20 estates was strikingly similar to those of social housing residents across estates' local authorities and at national level (Figure 29). The vast majority of estates also had lower unemployment, lower inactivity and higher employment rates than average for social housing in their areas.

Figure 29: Economic status of residents aged 16–74, 2001

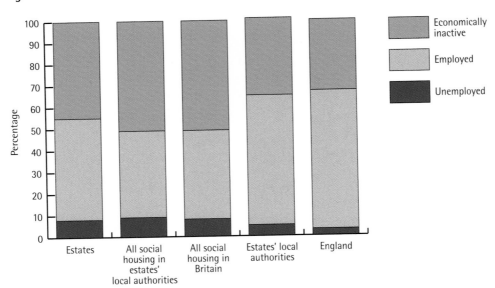

Note: Unemployment is shown here as a proportion of all residents aged 16–74, rather than of economically active residents as in Figure 28.
Source: 2001 census

Changes in age and household type

In 1981, 31% of estate residents were under 16; in 1991, the figure was 31% again, but, by 2001, it had fallen slightly to 29%. People under 24 made up 49% of the total populations in 1981, 45% in 1991 and 43% in 2001. These changes brought the estate populations slightly closer to the national and local age structures.

The proportion of estate residents of pension age fell from 13% in 1981, below the national and local authority levels, to 12% in 1991 and 9% in 2001, moving the estates further from the national age structure. Several managers mentioned difficulty finding residents for some sheltered accommodation or bungalows designated for older residents (estates 18, 20). Residents also commented on this process: "The estate has changed immensely now the older people have gone, the people they have brought in don't have the same care for the place, not the community spirit" (estate 5). Overall, these changes meant that slightly higher proportions of the estate population were of potential working age in 2001 than in 1991 or 1981.

The proportion of estate households made up of a lone parent with dependent children rose sharply between 1981 and 1991, from 9% to 18%. The sharp increase in this household type, often poor and facing childrearing challenges, was cause for concern. However, the figure fell slightly to 17% in estates by 2001, close to the figure of 15% for social housing across Britain and despite rises in local authorities and nationwide (Figure 30).

Figure 30: Lone-parent households with dependent children as a percentage of all households

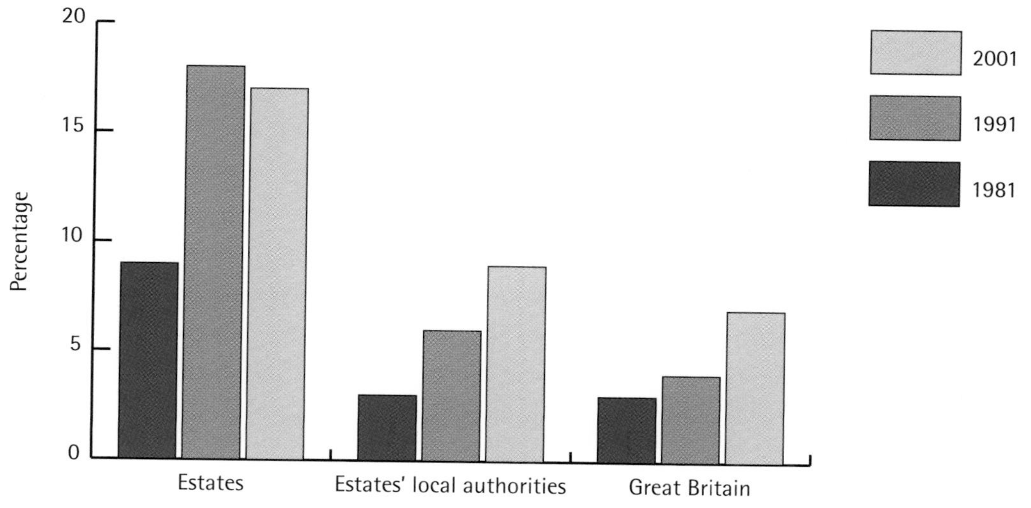

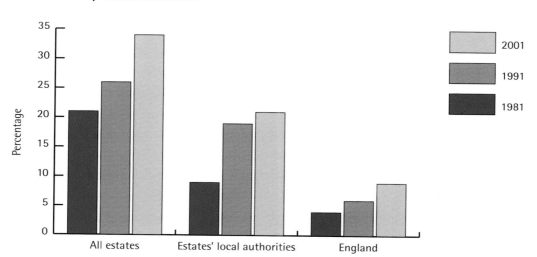

Sources: 1981, 1991, 2001 censuses. Comparable data not available for England alone.

Residents' ethnicity

On average, across the estates the proportion of residents who defined themselves as of non-white ethnicity rose from 26% in 1991 to 34% in 2001. Some estates that had had a figure of 1% or 2% minority ethnicity in 1991 saw an increase of a few percentage points by 2001 (but one that amounted to a doubling or tripling of the earlier figure), but the biggest percentage increases were in estates that already had an established mi nority population in 1991. In 2001, in seven estates the majority of the population was of non-white ethnicity (Figure 31).

Figure 31: Minority ethnic residents

Note: Figures for 1981 are for people in households headed by someone born in the New Commonwealth or Pakistan and for 1991 and 2001 are for people not of White British ethnicity.
Sources: 1981, 1991, 2001 censuses

By 2001, residents of Black African ethnicity, often born abroad, formed a bigger group than Black Caribbeans, mostly born in the UK, on most London estates. There were also substantial numbers and percentages of 'White: Other' (not White British or White Irish) residents, and managers mentioned people of Turkish Kurdish, Portuguese and Spanish origin. The split in ethnic mix between estates largely reflects regional population differences.

Over the period of the study, the estates divided into two groups: those with minority ethnic populations well below the national average and those well above it. In 2001, all five estates with at least 95% White residents were in the Midlands or the North, while the highest White population for an estate in London was 59%. However, the figures suggest that the very first minority ethnic households in some estates were joined by handfuls more over the 1990s. Where a large proportion of residents were minorities in 1991, the proportion increased further by 2001.

In 1991, ethnic minorities were over-represented in estates compared with local authority populations in 10 cases, and by 2001 this was true for 13. This appears to reflect the disadvantage in the housing market not only of foreign-born minorities but also of UK-born or longer-resident minorities. However, people of Asian ethnicity were sharply under-represented in most cases compared with their presence in local authority populations, even where these groups were disadvantaged, possibly due to fears of harassment.

Reactions to the pioneering minorities in formerly almost entirely white populations varied: "I'm not being racist but I think we have a few more immigrants than we deserve" (resident, estate 5, 99% White). In the 'majority minority' estates, effectively all groups were in the minority but residents still expressed concern about change: "We had community spirit but that's been taken out of it ... lots of Eastern bloc people, and they don't integrate ... white people and Afro-Caribbeans have given up and stick to people they know" (estate 9, 45% White). A fifth of residents interviewed said that racial harassment was a problem, well above the national average figure, and including those from different ethnic groups and from estates with high and low minority ethnic populations (Figure 21).

Poor health

In every age group, estate residents were more likely than others in their local authorities and in England to report in 2001 that their general health was 'not good', and to have a long-term illness, health problem or disability that limited daily activities or work (Figures 32, 33). The gap was particularly high for people in their fifties, who were twice as likely to be in 'not good' health as those in England generally.

One estate received Health Action Zone funding (Figure 17), recognising need, but residents' health in 2001 was no different from other estates (estate 12).

The poor health of estate residents is likely to partly explain the high and rising level of economic inactivity over the 1980s and 1990s. One fifth of all economically inactive residents said they did not work because of permanent sickness or disability.

Figure 32: Residents whose health was 'not good', by age group, 2001

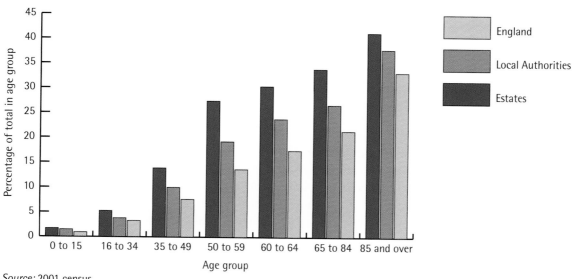

Source: 2001 census

Figure 33: Residents with limiting long-term illness, by age group, 2001

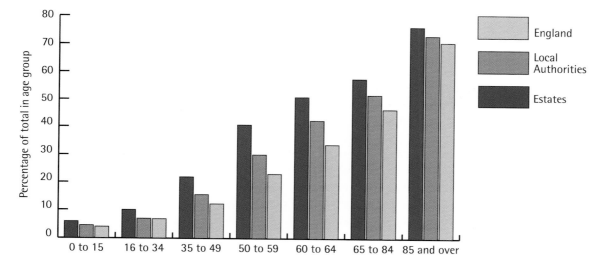

Source: 2001 census

Changes for individuals or changes in the mix of individuals?

Changes in the characteristics of estate residents, evident from the censuses between 1991 and 2001, were partly due to changes in the status of individual residents, which appear mainly to be due to national and regional economic trends:

- Changes in the overall demand for labour, reflecting national economic trends and enabling residents to move into employment, seem to be the most important explanation. Nationwide, unemployment was only 5% in 2001 compared with 9% in 1991. In addition, 11 of the estates are in London, where unemployment rates fell particularly sharply in the 1990s. Residents of London estates were also less likely to be economically inactive. However, the estates were not only able to benefit from the rising economic tide of the 1990s, but actually saw more change than their local authorities.

- The 1991 and 2001 censuses both occurred at times of rising employment but at slightly different points in the economic cycle. Poorer neighbourhoods tend to be affected early by rises in unemployment and late by falls. In 1991, employment growth had had only a few years to reach these estates but in 2001 employment had been growing for eight years.
- Slightly higher proportions of the estate population were of potential working age in 2001 than in 1991 or 1981. However, levels of economic inactivity among those aged 16-74 in the estates actually rose during the 1990s, against local and national trends, which suggests that some people were having difficulty finding employment despite jobs growth, and withdrew from the labour market (Figure 28).
- In two estates, residents got jobs in regeneration programmes. Numbers were small, although this had a big effect for the individuals and on residents and staff who knew them: "It's a joy to see that, it makes a real change" (resident, estate 3). Most estates did not have any special employment or training projects (Figure 17), although nationwide programmes such as the New Deal for the unemployed may have had an effect.

The changes in the population characteristics were also due to changes in the mix of individuals in the estates, linked to national and estate-level housing and regeneration policy:

- Existing residents in employment were being anchored via the Right to Buy and new residents in employment were brought into estates via mixed-tenure redevelopment (Figures 7, 9). The introduction of new home owners into the estate is not sufficient, however, to explain the changes in employment levels, even assuming that all home owners were employed. While the estates with large unemployment drops over 1991-2001 include some with major tenure change in the period (estates 13, 15, 18), large drops were also seen in estates that had no redevelopment and only small increases in the take-up of the Right to Buy (estate 3).
- The 2002 Homelessness Act and associated legislation removed some areas of discretion introduced under the previous government and increased the number of homeless priority needs groups for whom councils had a housing duty. The expected effect would have been to increase the concentration of homeless households – among which unemployment, inactivity, lone parenthood and children were over-represented – particularly in less popular estates. Some landlords felt this was happening to some extent (estate 9).
- However, this effect appeared to have been outweighed by improved social conditions nationwide and increased demand for social housing, including from more advantaged residents, for example, those who were employed but priced out of house purchase. Given that the estates were no longer highly stigmatised or detached from wider markets (Figure 6), this would have the opposite effect to the point above, increasing the proportion of more advantaged residents coming into the estates.
- In a minority of estates, landlords had altered allocations policies after 2000 to limit high concentrations of children, which had been seen as a problem.
- Variation in child population between the estates was closely connected to size of homes, largely fixed when the homes were built (see Table 1).
- The estates were also affected by the demographic transition process, as a generation of tenants who came into social housing in its post-war expansion phase aged and died.
- Population movement associated with redevelopment, and changes in management policy to increase the use of evictions for rent arrears and anti-social behaviour, may have had the effect of displacing some unemployed and disadvantaged residents to other areas. For example, one redeveloped estate was the subject of an unusual study

that found that only a fifth of original residents were in the estate after redevelopment, which took years to complete (estate 12). Evictions occurred across the 20 estates but numbers affected were much lower than those affected by redevelopment and were too small to explain the dramatic change in employment levels.

- Changes in ethnic mix reflect population movements. Global processes of economic and political change and conflict have undoubtedly been influential. In addition, the 1999 Asylum and Immigration Act, which sought to disperse asylum seekers and refugees outside London and the South East, has resulted in new minority households moving into several estates that previously had very small minority populations.

- Local policy has also had an impact where landlords have made concerted efforts to address racial harassment in estates that previously had limited minority populations and to open up choice: "We make it very clear now that there's nowhere in the city people can't live…. The mix of ethnicities on the estate is unheard of. Some even come here through choice now" (manager, estate 16, 95% White).

- There was no substantial evidence that health problems were caused by residence in the housing estates. Instead, it seems more likely that people in worse health, like other forms of disadvantage, were more likely to get access to social housing and to these estates. Most of the landlords, for example, gave priority on grounds of health needs or disability, although this alone would not explain the whole pattern.

Finally, some very small changes in the census between 1991 and 2001, including slightly lower response rates and the switch from Enumeration Districts to the slightly larger Output Areas, are likely to mean that small areas data for 2001 detected concentrations of deprivation very slightly less well than those for 1991. However, this cannot explain more than a fraction of the changes seen.

In summary:

- **The worsening of estate resident unemployment and other measures associated with disadvantage seen from 1981-91 was reversed over the period 1991-2001.**
- **The socioeconomic gaps between the estates and their local authorities and the nation identified in previous studies have been reduced, particularly in terms of unemployment rates, although all 20 estates still had higher levels of unemployment and economic inactivity than their local authorities and 19 had higher concentrations of children.**
- **Economic inactivity was an exception, increasing in the estates in 1991-2001 and diverging from local authority and national patterns.**
- **The changes were partly due to the changing status and circumstances of individuals and partly due to changes in the mix of individuals in the estates. They were the result of a complex mix of national policy, local factors and the social and economic context.**
- **The estates, as places, have benefited from the strong economy and increases in employment seen across the UK since 1995.**

Assessing progress

17. Improvements, 1980–95 and further gains, 1995–2005

Evidence from the previous chapter supports staff and residents' initial assessments that there had been further progress on the estates in the period 1995-2005 (Figures 1, 2 and 3).

Over the last 10 years of the study period, the 20 estates, as places, continued to make progress on some of the characteristics that had first sparked management initiatives

Table 5: Changes in estate characteristics leading to the establishment of estate-based management initiatives, by 1995 and by 2005

Characteristics	Start of initiatives in the late 1970s and early 1980s	1995	2005
Neglected, rubbish-strewn environment	20	1	0
Poor repairs and maintenance	19	7	5[1]
High level of crime and vandalism	19	9	4[2]
Rent arrears above local authority average for council housing	16	13	NA
Lone-parent households higher than local authority average	16	20	20
Unemployment and benefit claimancy higher than local authority average	16	20	20
Difficult to let	15	5	0
Proportion of children higher than local authority average	15	20	19
Proportion of homes empty above local authority average for council housing	14	10	6
Little community involvement	14	7	10[3]
Isolated location with few shopping or social facilities	11	11	11
Structural problems	10	6	1
Minority ethnic population higher than local authority average	9	10	13
Difficult to manage and unpopular design	7	6	1
Continuing stigma of first allocations from slum clearance areas	6	5	0

Notes:

[1] Local managers said service was worse than in other estates with the same landlord, or residents' group members, or a majority of street interviewees or housing managers, said that the repairs service had got worse over the past two years.

[2] Residents' group members, or a majority of street interviewees or housing managers, said that either crime or vandalism was a 'serious problem'.

[3] Lacked an active group recognised by the landlord, with a focus on housing management, and with more than three regular members.

NA = Not available. Population data relate to 1991 and 2001.

Sources: Power, 1984; Power and Tunstall, 1995; interviews, 2005

(Table 5). Some of the negative characteristics had entirely disappeared by 2005: for example, none of the estates had neglected rubbish-strewn appearances, none was 'difficult to let', and at last memories of 1930s slum clearance had faded. In addition, almost all of the structural and design problems had been dealt with through investment and demolition. However, in 2005, the estates continued to stand out from the social composition of their wider local authority areas.

Evidence from the previous chapter also supports the description of individual estates' trajectories based on staff and residents' initial assessments. Six of the 20 estates had had ongoing positive trajectories, with improvements in 1988-95 followed by more improvements or by stability over the period 1995-2005 (estates 1, 2, 3, 4, 5, 6). Ten more had experienced some threats or reverses to progress during the period, but by 2005 had seen further and secure improvement on the 1995 position (estates 7, 8, 9, 10, 11, 12, 13, 14, 15, 16). In the remaining four, the position in 2005 was uncertain (estates 17, 18, 19, 20).

18. Closing the gaps on local and national averages

In 1998, the Neigbourhood Renewal Unit pledged to end gaps between different areas so that 'within 10-20 years, no-one should be seriously disadvantaged by where they live' (SEU, 2001, p 8). The gaps between the estates and local and national comparators have reduced on some of the government's key targets for neighbourhood renewal (Table 6).

Table 6: Progress on key neighbourhood renewal targets

	Reduced gap between estates and social housing nationwide?	Reduced gap between estates and the local authorities in which they are located?	Reduced gaps between estates and nation?	Period
Employment	No gap 2001 – estates had higher employment	✓	✓	1991-2001
Crime	Not available	Not clear – both have reduced	Not clear – both have reduced	1995-2005
Education	Not available	✓	✓	1995-2005
Health	Not available	Gap exists	Gap exists	2001

The estates have reduced gaps with their local authorities and the nation as a whole on two neighbourhood renewal target areas, employment and education. Estate-based information on crime cannot be compared with wider areas as it is qualitative, but estate trends were moving in the same direction as local and national ones. There is no trend information on health.

There has also been progress in reducing gaps between estates and local authorities and the nation according to other measures (Table 7).

Table 7: Progress on related measures

	Reduced gap between estates and social housing nationwide?	Reduced gap between estates and the local authorities in which they are located?	Reduced gaps between estates and nation?	Period
Popularity	✓	✓	✓	1980–2005
Home ownership	No gap 2005 – estates included home ownership	✓	✓	1980–2005
Physical condition of homes	✓	✓	Not available	1980–2005
Housing management performance	✓	✓		1980–2005
Unemployment	No gap 2001 – estates had lower unemployment	✓	✓	1991–2001
Economic inactivity	No gap 2001 – estates had lower inactivity	✖ (increased)	✖ (increased)	1991–2001
Concentrations of typically low-income or non-earning households and residents (lone-parent households, under 16s and over 65s)	Not available	✓	✓ (except for over 65s)	1991–2001
General appearance, cleanliness and maintenance of homes and environment	✓	✓	✓	1980–2005

These are very positive outcomes. The process of polarisation between estates and wider areas on social conditions, service quality and life chances seems to be being reversed, and estates are becoming more 'normal' when compared with their local authorities, social housing nationwide, and the nation as a whole.

Despite these mainly positive trends, however, there were still gaps between the estates, their local authorities and the nation, and these gaps were still significant. The 20 estates have become more 'normal' as areas where the majority of homes are social rented. The 20 estates have come closer to the national average for social housing estates in terms of their:

- Mix of landlords (some Registered Social Landlord [RSL] as well as council new build and stock transfer)
- Levels of Right to Buy sales
- Management organisation and intensity
- Management policies
- Empty homes rates
- Management performance
- Built form (fewer non-traditional designed estates and homes).
- House condition
- Appearance, cleanliness and maintenance of homes and estates
- Extent of tenant involvement
- Overall estate popularity

By 2005, they were close to the national average for social housing tenants in terms of:

- Residents' satisfaction with their homes
- Residents' satisfaction with their landlord
- Residents' satisfaction with their area
- Residents' employment, unemployment and economic activity rates

However, at the same time, council and social housing has become much more of a minority tenure in 2005 than it was in 1980. In 1979, over 5 million English households rented from the council, making up 29% of all households. By 2004, the national stock of council homes in England had been cut in half, due to national policy, including sale to residents under the Right to Buy and other schemes, demolition without replacement, and from the late 1980s, transfer to housing associations. The remaining 2.3 million council homes made up just 11% of the total, while social housing including housing association homes totalled 4 million or 19% of all households. Estimates and measures of the amount of 'problematic' social housing are not robust enough to provide comparable information over time, but as more attractive homes and estates have been increasingly sold through the Right to Buy and the council sector has shrunk, the remaining 'problematic' social housing has become more typical and has loomed larger as a fraction of the total, while the deprivation of residents has increased. Home ownership is the national social norm, and social renting is less and less 'normal'. In 1981, the Survey of English Housing (ODPM, 2005, table S464) showed that more heads of social renting households were employed (47%) than economically inactive (45%), but by 2004, 31% were employed and more than twice as many, 63%, were inactive. Some commentators have argued this leaves social housing outdated, like black and white TV. Others argue that this means its role is more important, as well as more difficult. In either case, it makes the experience of these 20 estates more relevant to social housing overall.

There is a huge academic debate over whether and how areas 'create disadvantage': areas with concentrations of deprived people or crime might be explained by processes that push disadvantaged people into them or that attract criminals. However, if it was true in 1980 that the estates were significantly disadvantaging the people who live in them, it was still true in 2005. The experience of the 25 years of the study period shows that it is possible to make progress over the long term, but warns that closing the gaps enough to end 'significant disadvantage' is likely to take more than the '10 or 20 years' the Labour government has given itself.

In summary:

- **Improvements made in 1980-95 have been maintained, and there have been further gains from 1995 to 2005.**

- As a result, most of the gaps between the estates and their local authorities and the nation identified in previous studies have been reduced.
- The gaps between economic inactivity rates in the estates and in their local authorities and the nation increased.
- Gaps on many other measures have reduced but not disappeared.
- The estates have moved towards the average for social housing, but social housing has moved away from the local authority and national averages.

19. Explaining the changes

The changes in the estates are due to a complex combination of interacting changes in the estates themselves, in the surrounding local authorities and regions, and the nation as a whole. The changes can be attributed both to policy – a mix of mainstream housing policy and other policies targeted at less popular social housing estates or deprived areas – and to wider social and economic change.

Table 5 showed that between 1980 and 1995, progress was seen particularly on measures that could be affected by local housing management, an element of local policy. Capital investment, through national and local policy was also important. However, some social indicators worsened, due to wider social and economic change and the indirect effects of national policy, which reduced the size of social housing over the period.

Discussion in Chapter II showed that between 1995 and 2005, national and regional social and economic change had further important effects on the 20 estates:

- Higher employment and lower unemployment rates
- Improved educational performance
- Higher house prices
- Reduced crime

Lower economic inactivity rates, however, did not feed through to the estates.

Mainstream national housing policy had important effects:

- Right to Buy began to have significant direct effects, although still had much less effect than nationwide – the indirect effects on demand and characteristics of applicants were probably more significant.
- The estates were included in some pioneering urban whole stock transfers, and, with seven out of 20 estates affected by Arm's Length Management Organisations, they were also at the forefront of this development.
- Best Value had significant effects on estates through the reorganisation and improved performance of housing management.
- National housing policy targeted on less popular estates also continued to be important, through regeneration schemes that funded estate redevelopment.

Local policy – made by local authorities and RSLs, in many cases in reaction to central government encouragement and pressure – had the following effects:

- Estate ownership change and management change
- Prioritisation for regeneration funding
- Decisions not to maintain local offices
- Management centralisation and management policy shifts, including a focus on key performance indicators and anti-social behaviour, and support for resident involvement

However, they appeared to be less important than wider social and economic trends and national policy.

In 1995, the three factors that appeared to be crucial in explaining improvements overall and individual estate trajectories were targeted regeneration and investment through national and local policy, local housing management through local policy, and resident activism. In 1995, 17 of the 20 estates had at least two of the following three measures in place: an estate office, an active residents' group, and spending from more than one central government regeneration programme. In 2005, only 11 out of the 20 had two or more factors, even after further central government generation funding (Figure 17), and three estates had none. The salience of these factors also appeared to be in decline. When local managers were asked to assess progress over the 10 years to 2005, there was less emphasis given to housing management and resident involvement than in 1995. The three factors were still linked to improved trajectories, but less strongly than in 2005, as several of the redeveloped estates did not have local housing offices or active resident groups. Landlords and residents felt these two factors were needed less after improvements, although the sustainability of improvements will only be evident in time.

In summary:

- **Mainstream housing policy had direct effects on the estates, particularly over the last 10 years of the study, through changes in ownership and management and regeneration and investment, and has also had indirect effects through the residualisation of social housing generally.**
- **Policies targeted at less popular estates had very important effects throughout the period but their influence may have been in decline as estates became more 'normal' and lost special status.**
- **The estates have also benefited from the strong economy and housing markets seen across the UK since 1995.**
- **The prevalence of local housing management and resident involvement has reduced, and their salience in explaining changes may have reduced too.**
- **Overall, more weight must be given to factors beyond estates and local policy – national policy and social and economic conditions – in explaining changes over the decade 1995-2005 than in earlier periods.**

20. Have the estates 'turned the tide'?

Government policy hopes to make communities, both new and old, 'sustainable' – secure from the emergence or re-emergence of social, economic or physical problems that may create knock-on effects, and eventually require difficult and costly policy intervention.

Are the changes substantial and irreversible enough to have made these estates 'sustainable communities' by 2005? The extent of change has been described above. Over 25 years, the 20 estates have recovered from the most severe problems, partly due to policy intervention. However, the processes of change were not straightforward and were ongoing in 2005. Fourteen of the estates experienced at least some threats or reverses to progress during the period, and in 2005, four faced uncertain futures, after past initiatives did not achieve significant and sustained improvement (estates 17, 18, 19, 20).

In 1995, it seemed that achievements in many of the estates were being threatened by social polarisation. Over the subsequent 10 years, those trends altered due to a combination of economic change and direct and indirect effects of policy, which changed the characteristics of the population and affected the mix of people arriving in social housing and in the 20 estates. However, it is now possible that recent achievements in these estates could be threatened by 'normalisation'. New landlords and management organisations are as yet not tried and tested, and with lower priority for these estates within their landlord organisations, less local management and resident involvement, improvements could be eroded or estates made vulnerable to crises. In addition, some of the changes in estates since 1995, including increased popularity and tenure mix, were at least partly dependent on wide social and economic trends, including rising employment, increasing house prices and demand for social housing, falling crime and rising educational achievement. These may not all be sustainable. It is possible – in fact, likely – that if these trends change, the estates will be affected earlier or worse than other areas. As one senior manager said: "The market is changing faster than ever before … it has changed in one way [more demand] over the last three to four years, but it could change in another way in the future" (estate 18). In this situation, spirals of decline could set in again, and falling demand could threaten management performance and safety, and threaten any mixed tenure redevelopments.

In 1998, the Social Exclusion Unit suggested that some neighbourhoods were suffering from 'initiative-itis' after years of successive regeneration initiatives (SEU, 1998). However, the 20 estates appear to have received benefit from repeated and ongoing interventions, from capital investment to resident involvement. Strategic approaches to reinvestment across social housing through the Decent Homes Standard and the transfer of ownership and management structures offer the potential for a more efficient and less incremental approach. However, in addition, given increasingly strategic and stock-wide approaches, there may be a need to ensure a continued policy profile for less popular estates and more vulnerable residents, to ensure equal outcomes and sustainability of benefits.

Could mixed tenure or mixed-income redevelopment protect estates and neighbourhoods permanently from spirals of decline? The changes in the estates over the period 1980-2005 include, and were partly driven by, the fact that they have become more mixed in tenure and economic status. Redevelopment and mixing initiatives were able to – and even likely to, end the relative unpopularity of particular homes and estates, and to do so sustainably – if they were in regions or periods with higher housing demand. However, where demand for social housing and low-cost home ownership is low across a region, even estates that already have attractive housing, or have received major investment and offer a range of tenures, cannot necessarily escape from low relative popularity and the problems that go with it. In these circumstances, as one case out of the 20 shows, mixed tenure can even become a problem rather than a protection as homes in new tenures fail to find their expected market. In addition, dramatic redevelopment is costly and disruptive, and many – or even most – of the original residents may not stay in the estates to see any benefits. On the other hand, the experience of the 20 estates shows that, in the long term, and in a good economic environment, even relatively unpopular estates can achieve more social mix. This can occur after dramatic and more modest redevelopment, as well as through more gradual and diverse improvement initiatives and increased popularity. These gradual processes may offer more benefits to existing residents, including those on low incomes.

21. Cautions for interpretation and policy implementation

The cost and benefit of changes

This study has not attempted a full costing of the initiatives in estates, in comparison with 'do nothing' options or the situation for other estates in the local authorities or in the nation overall. Benefits have also not been fully quantified or compared to alternatives. Data and methodological problems make this close to impossible in retrospect. The succession of initiatives in estates were often developed or chosen pragmatically by central government, local authorities and residents given short- and medium-term political and financial pressures. The fact that benefits were produced does not mean that these initiatives were the only ones that could have been used or that they offered best value.

The impact of changes in the 20 estates on other neighbourhoods

In considering policy implications, the 20 estates cannot be seen in isolation. In some ways, these 20 less popular estates have gained at the expense of other estates and neighbourhoods. Obviously, there is the opportunity cost of the regeneration funding and the priority and attention they have received that then could not go to other areas. In addition, as the estates have become more popular, the status of 'least popular' and the stigma it attracts is passed on to others, even if objective conditions improve across the board. If population change in the 20 estates is partly due to existing or potential residents of the 20 estates being diverted elsewhere, this will affect other estates or neighbourhoods. On the other hand, some of the 20 have had to wait while other local estates have received funding and attention. In addition, over the period 1980-2005, the estates have been used to develop ideas that have been passed round local authorities and even nationwide, to benefit other areas.

The impact on places versus the impact on people

This study has concentrated on places, not the individuals within them. Even if these estates have turned the tide, we cannot be sure that the lives of all – or even most – individuals who have spent time living in them have changed for the better, let alone significantly or sustainably. One of the classic problems in neighbourhood research is the potential for getting the fortunes of neighbourhoods and the fortunes of individuals confused. The censuses provide snapshot views of the experience of groups whose membership only partly overlaps over 10 years. Improvement in areas may not mean improvements for individuals, and may have been generated by changing the mix of individuals in the areas. Some interviewees had lived in the estates all their lives, or since the estate had been built, and in one case a woman who had grown up in the estate said that not only her parents but also her grandparents had lived there. On the other hand, at each stage of the research, at least some of the estates had population turnover of more than 10% per year. In addition, estates subject to major redevelopments can undergo huge changes in population. Even if residents are granted the right to return after major refurbishment or demolition and new build, many do not. Overall, change between censuses should not be interpreted as change in the circumstances of individuals. While the overall circumstances for those living in the estates in 2005 appear better on many measures than they were in 1994 and better still than in 1980, it is possible that the personal situation of at least some members of earlier generations of residents has not improved or has even got worse.

Bibliography

Association of London Government (2003) *Briefing: Right to Buy and the impact on regeneration schemes*, London: Association of London Government.

Burbidge, M., Wilson, S., Kirby, K. and Curtis, A. (1981) *An investigation into difficult to let housing*, London: DoE.

CACI Ltd (2005) *ACORN: The smarter consumer classification*, London: CACI Ltd.

DCLG (Department for Communities and Local Government) (unpublished) Survey of English Housing, table S709, live table (www.communities.gov.uk/pub/184/S709Excel20Kb_id1155184.xls).

DETR (Department for the Environment, Transport and the Regions) (1997) *English Housing Condition Survey 1996*, London: DETR.

Dodd, T., Nicholas, S., Povery, D. and Walker, A. (2004) *Crime in England and Wales 2003/04*, Home Office Statistical Bulletin 10/04, London: Home Office.

Home Office (2005) *Integration matters: A national strategy for refugee integration*, London: Home Office.

IPPR (Institute for Public Policy Research) (2000) *Housing united: The final report of the IPPR forum on the future of social housing*, London: IPPR.

Lupton, R. (2003a) *Neighbourhood effects: Can we measure them and does it matter*, CasePaper 73, London: London School of Economics and Political Science.

Lupton, R. (2003b) *Poverty street*, Bristol: The Policy Press.

ODPM (Office of the Deputy Prime Minister) (2003a) *English House Condition Survey: Key results 2003*, London: ODPM.

ODPM (2003b) *Sustainable communities: Building for the future,* London: ODPM.

ODPM (2004) *Housing in England 2002/03: A report principally from the 2002/03 Survey of English Housing*, London: ODPM.

ODPM (2005) *Housing in England 2003/04 Part 1: Trends in tenure and cross tenure topics*, London: ODPM/National Statistics.

Power, A. (1984) *Local housing management: A Priority Estates Project survey*, London: Department of the Environment.

Power, A. (1991) *Running to stand still: Progress in local management on twenty unpopular council estates*, London: Priority Estates Project.

Power, A. and Tunstall, R. (1995) *Swimming against the tide: Progress and polarisation on 20 unpopular council estates in England*, York: Joseph Rowntree Foundation.

Price Waterhouse (1997) *Mapping local authority estates using the 1991 index of local conditions*, London: Department for the Environment, Transport and the Regions.

Ravetz, A. (2001) *Council housing and culture: The history of a social experiment*, London: Routledge.

Rhodes, J., Tyler, P. and Brennan, A. with Duffy, B. and Williams, R. (2002) *Evaluation of the Single Regeneration Budget Challenge Fund: Summary household survey results 1996-1999*, Discussion Paper 122, Cambridge: Department of Land Economy, University of Cambridge.

Smith, G.R. (1999) *Area-based initiatives: The rationale and options for area targeting*, CasePaper 25, London: London School of Economics and Political Science.

SEU (Social Exclusion Unit) (1998) *Bringing Britain together: A national strategy for neighbourhood renewal*, London: Cabinet Office.

SEU (2001) *A new commitment to neighbourhood renewal: National Strategy Action Plan*, London: Cabinet Office (www.neighbourhood.gov.uk/publications.asp?did=85).

Stephens, M., Whitehead, C. and Munro, M. (2005) *Lessons from the past, challenges for the future for housing policy: An evaluation of English housing policy 1975-2000*, London: Office of the Deputy Prime Minister.

Summerfield, C. and Gill, B. (eds) (2005) *Social trends no.35: 2005 edition*, Basingstoke: Palgrave Macmillan.

Thomasson, E. (2000) 'Small area statistics on-line', Paper presented at 'The census of population: 2000 and beyond' conference, Manchester, 22-23 June (www.ccsr.ac.uk/ conference/papers.htm, accessed July 2005).

Tunstall, R. (2003) '"Mixed tenure" policy in the UK: privatisation, pluralism or euphemism?', *Housing, Theory and Society*, vol 20, no 3, pp 153-9.

Appendix: Research methods

Overall, the four rounds of research on the 20 estates involved 225 visits to the estates and 241 in-depth interviews with staff and residents (Table A1).

In 2005, similar data were collected in similar ways to previous studies, to enable continued longitudinal comparison.

In 2005, for each estate, interviews were carried out with local housing managers and senior housing staff, such as directors of local authority housing departments or chief executives of Registered Social Landlords and Arm's Length Management Organisations (ALMOs). Where there was no local office and manager (Figure 12), the housing officer with the most knowledge about the estate was interviewed. In some estates where homes were no longer owned or managed by local authority staff (Figure 11), there were discussions with senior managers in the local authority as well as in the new organisation. Interviews with local housing managers took at least two hours, while those with senior managers and groups took at least one hour. Questionnaires used some questions from the Survey of English Housing and the British Crime Survey, so results for the estates and England could be compared. In a few cases, other estate-based workers were interviewed, including Police Community Support Officers, New Deal for Communities staff, a parish priest, community and tenant participation workers, and an ALMO board member.

Table A1: Total visits and interviews carried out, 1982–2005

	1982	1988	1995	2005
Estate visits	40	60	84	41
Residents' group member interviews	5 individuals	15 groups (totalling 54 individuals)	17 groups (totalling 131 individuals)	10 groups (totalling 58 individuals)
Street interviews with other residents	0	0	0	10 estates (totalling 89 individuals)
Local or neighbourhood manager interviews	20	20	20	19
Area or district manager interviews	0	0	9	20
Director, chief. executive or senior manager interviews[1]	18	18	14	12
Other estate-based worker interviews	0	0	16	8

Note: [1] The 20 estates are located in 18 local authorities.

In one case, the local authority did not want us to talk to its staff. The estate was undergoing dramatic redevelopment that had led to local controversy. In this case, use was made of extensive public information and informal contacts to piece together as much as possible of the factual information that staff would have provided.

In the 14 estates where there were residents' groups, they were approached for in-depth discussions. Eleven interviews were carried out, each lasting about an hour. There were problems making appointments in the remaining areas. In addition, in 10 estates, some with and some without residents' groups, very brief street interviews were carried out with about nine residents in each, totalling 89 individuals. Residents' groups tend to have more knowledge and involvement in housing policy and management, while the street interviews were more directly comparable with national surveys. Figures and discussion of results distinguish between residents who were group members and street interviews. Overall, residents' views were gathered for 16 of the 20 estates. Compared with the overall estate populations, tenants' group interviews slightly over-represented women, White residents, and those in their thirties and over fifty, while street interviewees over-represented people under 30 and minority ethnic residents.

In each round, interviewees were assured that neither the estates nor they as individuals would be identifiable from the research. This was intended to help gain access, to promote frankness, and to protect the areas from potentially stigmatising publicity.

In 2005, there were a total of 41 visits to the estates themselves, and a total of 158 interviews in the estates and at other locations. The number of estate visits was lower in 2005 than 1988 and 1995 because fewer staff are now estate-based and fewer interviews involved visits to estates themselves.

At each stage, the research made use of secondary data. In 2005, these included housing and regeneration strategy documents, Audit Commission inspection reports, newsletters, local newspaper reports, Ofsted schools data and the Survey of English Housing.

Housing management performance indicators used by most landlords differed between 1994 and 2005, which made direct comparison difficult. The characteristics of local staff had changed over the same period, with a reduction of typical time in post and narrowing of responsibilities, which meant that some quantitative information was harder to acquire and some anecdotal material not directly comparable.

Estate-linked schools, the schools that educated the greatest number of estate children, were identified from interviews and in some cases from direct contact with schools. Estate-linked schools do not necessarily educate a majority of estate children of secondary age and estate children do not necessarily form a majority of the students. In some cases, where local schools were single-sex or where schools appeared equally linked, more than one school was identified. Information was collected for 19 schools linked to 17 estates for 1994 and for 33 schools linked to 19 estates in 2004, apparently reflecting more complex admissions patterns. Checks showed that results were not significantly affected by increasing the base of schools and estates.

Information on estate residents was gathered from the censuses for 1981, 1991 and 2001. In each case, maps and information provided by interviewees were used to define the boundaries of the estates. Taking the smallest spatial units available for census data collection and publication, Enumeration Districts in 1981 and 1991 and Output Areas in 2001, small groups of these units were identified to best match the estate boundaries. Data were obtained for these areas and collated to provide data for the estates. Simple tests – checking the number of homes and the tenure mix against interview information – were carried out to ensure that the proxies were the best possible and would produce results that were reliable and comparable over time. Inevitably, the census data areas do not match area boundaries exactly, or in exactly the same way for each census. Any inaccuracies are likely to lead to slight underestimates of deprivation, by including homes and households that were not actually part of housing estates. This method is widely used, forming the basis of small area data via Neighbourhood Statistics.

In 1981, the census did not contain a question on ethnicity and researchers instead estimated minority ethnicity through counting people in households headed by someone born in the New Commonwealth or Pakistan, so data for 1981 and 1991 are not exactly comparable.

Some very small changes in the census between 1991 and 2001, including slightly worse response rates and the switch from Enumeration Districts to the slightly larger Output Areas, are likely to mean small area data for 2001 detected concentrations of deprivation slightly less well than those for 1991, and may slightly overestimate improvements for example, in employment, over the decade.